Cambridge Elements ≡

Elements in the Philosophy of Religion
edited by
Yujin Nagasawa
University of Birmingham

THE AXIOLOGY OF THEISM

Klaas J. Kraay
Ryerson University

CAMBRIDGE
UNIVERSITY PRESS

CAMBRIDGE
UNIVERSITY PRESS

University Printing House, Cambridge CB2 8BS, United Kingdom

One Liberty Plaza, 20th Floor, New York, NY 10006, USA

477 Williamstown Road, Port Melbourne, VIC 3207, Australia

314–321, 3rd Floor, Plot 3, Splendor Forum, Jasola District Centre, New Delhi – 110025, India

103 Penang Road, #05–06/07, Visioncrest Commercial, Singapore 238467

Cambridge University Press is part of the University of Cambridge.

It furthers the University's mission by disseminating knowledge in the pursuit of education, learning, and research at the highest international levels of excellence.

www.cambridge.org
Information on this title: www.cambridge.org/9781108742276
DOI: 10.1017/9781108592833

First published 2021

A catalogue record for this publication is available from the British Library.

ISBN 978-1-108-74227-6 Paperback
ISSN 2399-5165 (online)
ISSN 2515-9763 (print)

The Axiology of Theism

Elements in the Philosophy of Religion

DOI: 10.1017/9781108592833
First published online: September 2021

Klaas J. Kraay
Ryerson University

Author for correspondence: Klaas J. Kraay, kraay@ryerson.ca

Abstract: Theism is the view that God exists; naturalism is the view that there are no supernatural beings, processes, mechanisms, or forces. This Element explores whether things are better, worse, or neither on theism relative to naturalism. It introduces readers to the central philosophical issues that bear on this question, and it distinguishes a wide range of ways it can be answered. It critically examines four views, three of which hold (in various ways) that things are better on theism than on naturalism, and one of which holds just the opposite.

Keywords: God, atheism, naturalism, pro-theism, anti-theism

ISBNs: 9781108742276 (PB), 9781108592833 (OC)
ISSNs: 2399-5165 (online), 2515-9763 (print)

Contents

1 Stage-Setting

Here is a provocative question: does it *matter* whether God exists? This question is not about *whether*, in fact, God exists. Nor is it about the value of *belief* in God. Nor is it about the value of *religious practices* oriented toward God. So, what is it about? Well, one way to tackle it is to examine whether, on the view that God exists, things are better, worse, or neither. Taking this approach, our question transforms into this: "What *axiological difference* would – or does – theism make?" Notice that this new question is deliberately phrased to be neutral between two perspectives: that of someone who believes that God exists, and that of someone who does not believe that God exists.[1] The theist, of course, thinks that God does exist, and so when she poses this question, she asks what difference God's existence *really does* make. The nontheist, on the other hand, asks what difference God's existence *would* make, if God *were* to exist.

Like so many philosophical questions, this one is deceptively simple to pose, and enormously difficult to answer. In recent years, however, philosophers have begun to tackle it with vigor and rigor.[2] They have tried to assess, in various ways, the axiological import of God's existence, nature, and activity if theism is true, and, conversely, the axiological import of God's *non*existence, if theism is false. This topic has come to be known as the "axiology of theism."[3] This section sets the stage for the subsequent discussion. In Section 1.1, I set out five generic positions that one might take on this issue, and, in Section 1.2, I clarify some key terms. In Section 1.3, I introduce a distinction between wide and narrow versions of these generic positions, I discuss how different versions of them can (and cannot) be combined, and I introduce some alternative views. In Section 1.4, I discuss a challenge to the intelligibility of this inquiry, and, in Section 1.5, I briefly introduce key considerations that are (or could be) offered in favor of these five views. In Section 1.6, I set out the plan for the rest of this Element.

---

[1] The latter, of course, may be either an agnostic or an atheist. Moreover, the latter needn't be nonreligious: there are many nontheistic religions, after all.

[2] Although important themes from this discussion are anticipated in Rescher (1990), the contemporary literature on this topic begins with Kahane (2011). For surveys of most of the discussion to date, see Kraay (2018a) and Lougheed (2019).

[3] This term is infelicitous for two reasons. First, it might prompt the thought that broader questions about the relationship between God and value are at stake, whereas it really means to connote an investigation of the axiological consequences of theism, relative to some other worldview(s). Second, an important subsidiary thread has considered what preferences can be rational with respect to God's existence or nonexistence – and one point of dispute has been whether preferences must track axiological judgments in order to be rational.

1.1 Five Generic Positions

Here are five generic positions that one might take on this issue. I call them "generic" because, as we will see, they can be specified in various ways.

> GENERIC PRO-THEISM: Things are *better* on theism than on naturalism, and this is due to God's existence, nature, or activity.
>
> GENERIC ANTI-THEISM: Things are *worse* on theism than on naturalism, and this is due to God's existence, nature, or activity.
>
> GENERIC NEUTRALISM: Things are neither better nor worse on theism than on naturalism as a result of God's existence, nature, or activity.[4]
>
> GENERIC AGNOSTICISM: We should suspend judgment about what axiological difference God's existence, nature, or activity makes, relative to naturalism.
>
> GENERIC QUIETISM: The question of what axiological difference God's existence, nature, or activity makes (relative to naturalism) is unanswerable in principle.

These axiological positions are displayed on the horizontal axis of the table below. The positions on the vertical axis represent three basic views about *whether God exists*. (That's why I call them *existential* positions.)

Table 1 Combinations of existential and axiological positions

		GENERIC AXIOLOGICAL POSITIONS				
		Pro-theism	*Anti-theism*	Neutralism	Agnosticism	Quietism
EXISTENTIAL POSITIONS	Theism					
	Atheism					
	Agnosticism					

The point of bringing these together in a table is to illustrate clearly various combinations of existential and axiological positions. A familiar one is theistic pro-theism. Someone who holds these views believes that God exists, and also that, as a result, things are *better* than they would be on naturalism. Another common combination is atheistic anti-theism. Someone who holds these views believes that God does not exist, and also that if God *were* to exist, things would

---

[4] This, of course, is compatible with things being either better or worse on theism, relative to naturalism, for reasons that *do not* involve God's existence, nature, or activity.

be *worse* than on naturalism because of God's existence, nature, or activity. At first glance, it might seem that every cell in Table 1 represents a coherent combination of positions, but this has been contested.[5]

1.2 Clarification of Terms

The axiological positions above involve key terms like "theism," "naturalism," "things," "better," and "worse." These need to be clarified.

Let's begin with "theism." Evidently, the generic positions set out in Section 1.1 carry no commitment to any particular account of God's nature or activity. And of course, many different views about God have been proposed by philosophers, theologians, and others throughout history. This Element will generally concentrate on the following model of God: a personal being who is unsurpassable in power, knowledge, and goodness, who is the ultimate creator and sustainer of everything that contingently exists, whose essential nature is fixed, and who exists in every logically possible world.[6] This is an enormously important, influential – and controversial – model. But of course, one could undertake this sort of axiological investigation using other models of God, or indeed nontheistic worldviews.[7]

The view that such a being exists can be called *bare theism*.[8] It can be fleshed out in myriad ways, which we can call *expansions* of bare theism. Some of these are thought to be logically entailed by bare theism. For example, some have said that if bare theism were true, there would no evil at all. This consequence is thought to follow from the divine attributes, and so we can call views like this (putative) *logical expansions*. Other expansions of theism are not thought to be logical consequences; they are simply addenda. Consider, for example, the familiar idea that God sometimes performs miracles. Many expansions of bare theism of both types have been proposed, and, of course, many are enormously controversial.[9] In the rest of this Element, I generally concentrate

---

[5] Schellenberg (2018) and Tooley (2018) offer reasons for thinking that anti-theism entails atheism. For a survey of connections drawn in the literature between the existential and axiological issues, see Kraay (2018a: 18–19). See also Hendricks (2020) and the subsequent discussion in Lougheed (2020a).

[6] I will occasionally follow tradition by using masculine personal pronouns for God, but I do not mean to suggest thereby that God has either a sex or a gender. This definition of theism, evidently, makes neither claim.

[7] Discussions of other models of God by analytic philosophers can be found in Diller and Kasher (2013) and Buckareff and Nagasawa (2016). For efforts to broaden the axiological discussion to other worldviews, see Dumsday (2020) and the ensuing exchange with the other contributors in Lougheed (2020a), and see also Lougheed (2020b, chapters 7–10).

[8] An even more austere version of theism holds merely that God is the greatest possible being, without specifying what this involves.

[9] By this I mean that it's controversial whether the former are logical consequences of theism, and it's controversial whether the latter are plausible expansions.

on bare theism, but I will signal when I turn to various common and important expansions.

The next term is "naturalism." This is the view that there are no supernatural beings, processes, mechanisms, or forces. Most of the literature to date involves a comparative axiological evaluation of theism and naturalism. But, of course, *non*naturalistic, *non*theistic views could be compared to theism. Consider, for example, the view that there necessarily exists a being just like God except in one respect: instead of perfectly good, this being is perfectly *bad*. (It's enormously plausible to suppose that things are better in various ways on theism than on a worldview involving a malevolent deity.) I will follow the majority of the literature in comparing theism to naturalism.

Moreover, I will concentrate on a version of naturalism that denies that there are natural beings, processes, mechanisms, or forces that have the same axiological effects as God is thought to have. Here is an example. Pro-theists sometimes say that if theism is true, God ensures that ultimate justice will prevail, and anti-theists sometimes say that if theism is true, God violates our privacy. I will assume that, if naturalism is true, nothing likewise guarantees ultimate justice or universally compromises our privacy. After all, there is no scientific reason to suppose that any such being, processes, mechanisms, or forces exist on naturalism, so they can be set aside.[10]

The first three axiological positions speak rather loosely about God's existence, nature, and activity making "things" better or worse. But what are these things to which theism is held to make an axiological difference? To date, most of the literature has focused on value bearers like *the actual world* and *the lives of persons*.[11] Here are two examples. Some pro-theists argue that on theism, God's existence, nature, or activity ensures that the *actual world* is better than it would be on naturalism; meanwhile, some anti-theists argue that on theism, God's existence, nature, or activity ensures that the *lives of persons* are worse than they would be on naturalism. But these are not the only possible objects of axiological evaluation. More broadly, one could examine the axiological import of theism for a range of worlds, or even for the entirety of modal space (as I will do in Section 2). More narrowly, one could examine the axiological import of theism for a proper part of a world, for the lives of some group of persons, or the life of just one person, or even for one or more *segments* of a life or lives. It is

---

[10] Three discussions that are not restricted in these ways are Kahane (2018), Licon (forthcoming), and Lougheed (2020b, chapter 6).

[11] In the versions of theism I have in mind, God is considered a person as well. (Indeed, on Trinitarian variants of theism, God is considered *tri*-personal.) But in what follows, when I speak of persons, I will intend *non*divine persons, unless I note otherwise.

extremely important to be clear about which *value-bearing entity* is the object of one's axiological evaluation.[12]

Finally, these axiological positions are value judgments, and so one might wonder what sort of value is at issue. As we will see, philosophers in this discussion have generally focused on either the intrinsic or instrumental (dis) value of God's existence, nature, or activity, with respect to either the lives of persons, or the worlds they inhabit.

1.3 Scope Issues, Combining Positions, and Alternate Views

Once the relevant object of axiological evaluation is specified, an important distinction can be introduced. The generic positions of Section 1.1 can be understood *narrowly* or *widely*. The former concerns the axiological consequences of theism in *one or more respects only*, while the latter focuses on the *overall* axiological effects of theism for the relevant object of evaluation. Consider, for example, the actual world. A *narrow actual world anti-theist* thinks that the actual world is worse *in some respect(s)* on theism than on naturalism, whereas a *wide actual world pro-theist* thinks that the actual world is *overall* better on theism than on naturalism. As the object of axiological evaluation is specified, and as this distinction is applied, these views become specific, rather than generic.

Each of the five axiological views can be construed widely or narrowly. This means that there are thirty possible combinations of existential and axiological positions for each object of axiological evaluation. Some of these pairs can be held consistently with others. For example, consider an atheist who thinks that God's existence would make the lives of all persons better *in certain respect(s)*, but who is unsure about the *overall* axiological import of theism on the lives of all persons. With respect to this object of axiological evaluation (the lives of all persons), such an atheist would be both a *narrow pro-theist* and *wide agnostic*. But, clearly, not all combinations are compossible. For example, if one is a quietist in either the wide or narrow sense about some object of axiological evaluation, one cannot also be a pro-theist or anti-theist in the same sense about

---

[12] The literature has typically distinguished between *personal* and *impersonal* versions of these views. Unsurprisingly, the former have persons as their primary focus, while the latter do not. This distinction no longer strikes me as terribly helpful, so I will not rely on it here. Here is a quick rationale. One could hold, for example, that a *world* is overall good only if certain *person*-affecting requirements are met. (Perhaps, for instance, all persons must have lives that are on balance worth living in order for a world to be considered overall good.) Suppose a pro-theist holds that God ensures that all worlds that include persons are overall good. The object of axiological evaluation here is a world, not persons, so by that criterion the view is impersonal – but of course it centrally involves a person-affecting consideration. For further discussion of this distinction, see Mawson (2012).

the same object. And, of course, this is so regardless of what position one takes on the question of whether God exists.

Moreover, one can hold one axiological position with respect to one object of evaluation, and a different axiological position with respect to a different object of evaluation. For example, one might think that on theism, the *lives of certain persons* are worse than they would be on naturalism (either in some respect or overall), while holding that on theism, *worlds of a certain sort* are better than they would be on naturalism (either in some other respect or overall).

Generic pro-theism and anti-theism suggest that God's existence, nature, or activity *ensures* that things are better or worse, respectively, on theism than on naturalism. More modest variants of these positions hold that God's existence, nature, or activity *makes it likely* that things are better or worse. (Likewise, probabilistic variants of the remaining three positions could be devised.) In addition, some authors have focussed on whether it is *rational to prefer* that theism or naturalism is true, instead of on what axiological difference theism makes. Analogues of each of the five axiological positions can be devised that invoke rational preference.[13] Probabilistic variants of the axiological positions, and the views about rational preference, can also be construed narrowly or widely. The points I made about combining existential and axiological positions also apply to these, *mutatis mutandis*. In what follows I generally focus on nonprobabilistic axiological judgments.

To date, most work in this area has concerned pro-theism and anti-theism about the value of actual world and the lives of persons, based on an axiological comparison of theism and naturalism, and mostly expressed in nonprobabilistic terms. But, given the vast array of views distinguished here, and the ways they can be combined – and given that there are many alternatives to both theism and naturalism as I have construed them – it is clear that this discussion could be broadened in numerous ways.

1.4 Are the Relevant Comparisons Intelligible?

Theists often hold that God exists in *all* logically possible worlds. In other words, God's existence is *logically necessary*.[14] Indeed, this was part of the

---

[13] It is often assumed that what it is rational to prefer tracks one's axiological assessment, but this has been denied. For discussion of the literature on rational preference in this domain, see Kraay (2018a: 21–22).

[14] The points in this paragraph could also be expressed with reference to *metaphysical* possibility and necessity. For important discussions of how the distinction between logical and metaphysical possibility can be brought to bear in this debate, see Mawson (2012 and 2018). For complaints about construing God as logically necessary in this debate, see Moser (2013).

definition of bare theism in Section 1.2. Notice that on this view, there are no logically possible worlds *lacking* God available for axiological comparison. Nor, hence, are there any possible persons or lives on naturalism available for comparison. These worlds, persons, and lives are all strictly *im*possible. Likewise, naturalists often hold that God's existence is *logically impossible.*[15] If so, there are no logically possible worlds *including* God available for axiological comparison. Nor, hence, are there possible persons or lives on theism available for comparison. This seems to threaten the intelligibility of the comparative axiological project, since in either case, one of the putative comparates is impossible. There is a consensus in the literature that this challenge is not fatal, but none on how best to respond.[16] In this Element, I will follow a strategy first suggested by Kahane (2011: 36): I will focus on *epistemic possibilities*. This means that I will assume that both theism and naturalism are *true for all we know*, and I will then compare various epistemically possible worlds or states of affairs in which theism is true with various epistemically possible worlds or states of affairs in which naturalism is true.[17]

1.5 Considerations Supporting Each Generic Axiological View

As noted, most of the discussion has concentrated on various versions of pro-theism and anti-theism with respect to the actual world and the lives of persons. Here are six considerations offered in favor of *pro-theism*: on theism, God ensures that (a) ultimate justice prevails; (b) morality is anchored; (c) persons' lives are, or can be, meaningful; (d) there is no gratuitous evil; (e) involuntary, undeserved suffering ultimately benefits those who experience it; and that (f) most persons believe that God exists, which is a prerequisite for being able to enter into a relationship with God. And, of course, no equivalent guarantees are available on naturalism. Meanwhile, here are six considerations offered in favor of *anti-theism*: on theism, relative to naturalism, persons have significantly (a) less freedom, (b) less dignity, and (c) less privacy; and, moreover, (d) the world is less intelligible; (e) commonsense morality is compromised; and (f) some people's lives are rendered meaningless. I will discuss all twelve of these, and the interplay between them, in Section 4. For now I will simply note that, in

---

[15] For example, some hold that a pair of essential attributes of God is inconsistent. To think this is to hold that God, so construed, is logically impossible. For arguments in this vein, see Martin and Monnier (2003).

[16] For a survey of responses, see Kraay (2018a: 5–7). See also Oppy (2020) and the subsequent discussion in Lougheed (2020a).

[17] Of course, as Kahane says, this strategy is only open to those who do not take themselves to *know* that theism (or atheism) is true. Such individuals cannot, after all, deem the relevant alternative to be epistemically possible. If they wish to engage in this comparative axiological project, they will have to adopt a different strategy.

principle, the first six can be harnessed to support narrow or wide variants of pro-theism, while the second six can be harnessed to support narrow or wide variants of anti-theism, in both cases relative to various different objects of axiological evaluation.

One way to be a *neutralist* holds that, with respect to some object of axiological evaluation, the "upsides" of theism posited by pro-theists are precisely counterbalanced by the "downsides" posited by anti-theists, or that they are, in Ruth Chang's sense, "on par" (Chang 1997). A more radical way holds that there are no axiological consequences of God's existence, nature, or activity whatsoever. Neutralism has not been defended in the literature to date. It might, however, inform a view that has been discussed: *apatheism*.[18] The apatheist is apathetic about, or indifferent to, the question of whether God exists. If you think that God's (non)existence makes no axiological difference, you might thereby be led to apatheism.

The *agnostic* about this issue believes that we should suspend judgment about the axiological effects of God's existence, nature, or activity, relative to naturalism, with respect to some object of axiological evaluation. The *positive* agnostic judges that, given the available arguments and evidence, suspending judgment is the most reasonable thing to do. The *withholding* agnostic, on the other hand, simply withholds judgment, even about the statement "agnosticism is the most reasonable position."[19] Either version can be motivated by considering the difficulties involved in making the relevant comparisons.[20] Doubts about our abilities come in two basic types. First, one might doubt that we have the wherewithal to properly isolate and hold before our minds the relevant object(s) of evaluation. Second, one might doubt that we have the ability to properly grasp or assess the axiological import of the (putatively) value-adding and value-reducing consequences of theism, individually or jointly. The larger the object of evaluation is, the more plausible such concerns can seem.[21]

Finally, the *quietist* holds that, for some object of axiological evaluation, no intelligible comparison can be made. I mentioned one reason for this view previously: someone who holds that theism is logically necessary (or, alternatively, that theism is logically impossible) might believe that this *in principle*

---

[18] For discussions of apatheism, see Nelson (1996); Oppy (1998); Hedberg and Huzarevich (2017); Beshears (2019); and Citron (*ms.*).

[19] Thanks to Nathan Ballantyne for suggesting this distinction.

[20] The *modal skepticism* of Peter van Inwagen (1998) could be used to support this view. For a helpful introduction to pertinent issues in modal epistemology, see Vaidya (2015).

[21] For example, it might seem entirely beyond our ability to trace all the consequences, in a given world, of the truth of theism (or, for that matter, of the falsity of theism). And perhaps identifying them all, and evaluating their axiological import, both individually and jointly, *is* necessary in order to arrive an overall judgment of the axiological status of that world. For more on this, see Kraay (2018a: 7–9).

defeats any attempt to engage in comparative axiological analysis.[22] A different motivation for quietism involves incommensurability or incomparability. For example, someone who believes that all theistic worlds are overall incommensurable and incomparable with all naturalistic worlds might be inclined to think that no wide axiological comparison of such worlds is possible in principle.

1.6 Outline of this Element

In the rest of this Element, I largely set aside neutralism, agnosticism, and quietism about this axiological issue. This is because a central goal is to orient readers to the literature, and these views have not been discussed much to date. In Section 2, I examine the problems and prospects for an extremely ambitious form of pro-theism: *global wide modal space pro-theism*. This view holds that, considered in its entirety, modal space is overall better on theism than on naturalism.[23] In Section 3, I examine the problems and prospects for *wide actual world pro-theism*. This view holds that the actual world is overall better on theism than on naturalism. Finally, in Section 4, I examine *local modal space pro-theism* and *local modal space anti-theism*. The former holds that worlds that are relevantly and sufficiently similar to the actual world are *better* on theism than on naturalism, while the latter holds that these worlds are *worse* on theism than on naturalism. In each case, I aim to map the relevant terrain by charitably explaining the arguments for and against each position, and by showing how they connect to related philosophical and theological topics.

2 Global Modal Space Pro-theism

As I explained in Section 1, in order to analyze the axiological consequences of theism, one must first specify the object of one's axiological analysis. Most of the literature to date has focused on *the actual world* or the *lives of persons*, and I will consider these in Sections 3 and 4, respectively. Here, however, I consider something much larger: modal space in its entirety. In particular, I will examine this pro-theistic view:

> GLOBAL, WIDE MODAL SPACE PRO-THEISM (GWMSPT): Modal space is overall better on theism than on naturalism, and this is due to God's existence, nature, or activity.

---

[22] A robust defense of this view would presumably provide reasons why none of the proposed solutions to this problem are viable.

[23] The views in this paragraph all hold, of course, that the relevant axiological difference is due to God's existence, nature, or activity.

This view is *global* because it encompasses the entire sweep of modal space, rather than some region, and it is *wide* because it claims that theism makes modal space writ large better *overall*, rather than merely in some respect.[24]

So, why would anyone think that the existence, nature, or activity of God would (or does) make a positive axiological difference to modal space writ large? Let's begin with this: it is a familiar idea that if theism is true, certain states of affairs will not be actual. For example, it is widely held that if God exists, the actual world includes no *gratuitous evil*.[25] That's because, so the thinking goes, given God's knowledge, power, and goodness, God would prevent gratuitous evil from occurring in the actual world. But could God and gratuitous evil then coexist in some nonactual possible world? It seems not: the same rationale for thinking that God would prevent gratuitous evil in our world applies equally to other worlds. Moreover, since God is a necessary being, he exists in *every* possible world. The upshot is that if theism is true, there is no gratuitous evil in *any* possible world. In contrast, on naturalism, there is nothing to prevent gratuitous evil from occurring in many worlds. Indeed, naturalists typically believe that there is plenty of gratuitous evil in *our* world.

Here is the moral to draw from this example: if God exists, then some things that would otherwise have been possible are not possible. And here's a plausible corollary: if God exists, then some things that would otherwise *not* have been possible *are* possible. (A quick example: on theism, one might say, it is possible to *enter into a personal relationship* with God – but evidently this is impossible on naturalism.) Thomas Morris connects these complementary ideas by saying that God is "a delimiter of possibilities" (1987: 48); Brian Leftow connects them with the image of God's "modal footprint" (2005: 96, 2010: 30). The basic idea captured by these expressions is that modal space is *different* on theism than it is on naturalism. Now, the modal space *pro*-theist thinks that the axiological difference made by this delimitation or footprint is (or would be) *positive*. The *global, wide* modal pro-theist thinks that when one considers the *entire sweep* of modal space, it's reasonable to think that it is better *overall* on theism than on naturalism. Before turning to reasons that favor this view, I begin with some clarifications.

---

[24] One could, of course, devise *local* versions of modal space pro-theism: these focus on some region of modal space. (I will consider one such view in Section 4.) Equally, one could devise *narrow* versions of either global or local modal space pro-theism.

[25] An instance of evil is gratuitous if neither its occurrence, nor God's allowing it to occur, is needed to bring about a greater good. I discuss the pro-theistic import of this view, and some prominent criticisms of it, in Section 4.2.4.

2.1 Clarifications

(a) Initially, GWMSPT may seem incoherent. The view purports to compare modal space *on theism* to modal space *on naturalism* – and, as Brian Leftow notes, "[t]here are no possible alternatives to the entire framework of possible worlds: to be a possible alternative is just to be situated somewhere within it, and so the very concept of a *possible* alternative to that framework as a whole is incoherent" (2017: 161–162). But, following the strategy set out in Section 1.4, GWMSPT should be understood to compare two *epistemically possible accounts* of modal space, at most one of which is correct. I will call one *theistic modal space*, and the other *naturalistic modal space*.

(b) It can be tempting to think of modal space as an entity – a container for possible worlds, perhaps – that is the real value-bearer at issue. But as I will use the term, "modal space" is simply a way of speaking about the entire ensemble of worlds. Accordingly, GWMSPT is best construed as a comparative claim about the axiological status of this ensemble of worlds on two rival epistemically possible scenarios: theism and naturalism.

(c) There are many different accounts of what possible worlds are: for example, some deem them to be concrete objects; others say they are abstract objects; and still others hold them to be convenient fictions. In what follows, I will remain as neutral as possible between these views.[26]

(d) Philosophers of religion typically take for granted that possible worlds can exhibit both *absolute* and *relative* overall axiological status. In other words, they can properly be deemed *good* or *bad* simpliciter, and one world can properly be deemed *better* or *worse* than another. Moreover, these are held to be *objective* features. I will not defend this view here; I will simply take it on board.[27]

(e) Someone might worry that worlds are not the appropriate object of axiological evaluation in this discussion: perhaps what *really* matters is the axiological effects of theism on their *inhabitants*. In reply, one could

---

[26] For an introductory survey of this terrain, see Menzel (2016). Space does not permit an extended discussion, but one point is worth noting. In Sections 2.2, 2.3, and 2.4, I will discuss three ways to support GWMSPT. Some of the objections to each of these ways raise worries for the familiar idea that God chooses exactly one world to be actual. But these objections cannot be raised on David Lewis's (1986) modal realism, which denies precisely that any world enjoys a fundamentally privileged status relative to all the others. For an important defense of *theistic* Ludovician (i.e., Lewisian) modal realism, see Almeida (2017b, 2017c, and 2020a).

[27] For more, see Kraay (2008b). One philosopher who denies that worlds exhibit absolute axiological status is Rubio (2020).

simply posit a tight connection between the two. Of course, not all worlds include persons. But one could hold, for example, that no world that includes persons can be deemed good overall unless certain axiological requirements pertaining to those persons are satisfied. (Perhaps they must lead lives that are on-balance good, or meaningful, etc.) Likewise, one might argue that certain requirements on the lives of animals or other denizens must be met in order for the worlds they inhabit to be good overall.

(f) Examination of theistic modal space aims to ascertain the axiological consequences of God's existence, nature, and activity. For our purposes, God's existence is taken to be necessary, and God's nature is taken to be fixed. So in theistic modal space, every world includes God, and God's nature does not vary. But things are different with respect to God's *activity*, since it is traditionally held that God's actions are contingent. In other words, in theistic modal space, God acts (or refrains from acting) in some ways in some worlds, and in different ways in other worlds.

(g) I will soon discuss three ways to support GWMSPT, each of which makes claims about *all* possible worlds. But arguments for GWMPST needn't involve claims about all worlds. After all, this view merely asserts that theistic modal space as a whole is overall better than naturalistic modal space, and this is compatible with God's existence, nature, or activity ensuring that *only some specific region* of modal space is better than it would be on naturalism, either overall or in some respect(s).[28] Of course, such arguments bear the burden of showing that the axiological improvement in this region conferred by theism is sufficient to establish GWMSPT.[29]

In Sections 2.2, 2.3, and 2.4, I outline the prospects and problems for three ways to support GWMSPT. The first says that, on theism, every world is overall *unsurpassable*. The second says that, on theism, every world is overall *good*. The third says that, on theism, every world is overall *better than it would otherwise be*. The first is the most ambitious; the third is the most modest. In Section 2.5, I offer some final thoughts on GWMSPT.

---

[28] Analogy: the existence of a mountain in one region of geographic space makes the average elevation of the entire region higher than it would otherwise be.

[29] There are still other ways to defend GWMSPT. For example, one could argue that some or all worlds are better *in certain respects* on theism than on naturalism, and that these respects suffice to make modal space writ large better *overall*. I will not consider such arguments.

2.2 First Argument for GWMSPT: On Theism, Every World Is Overall Unsurpassable

Consider this proposition:

> EVERY WORLD UNSURPASSABLE (EWU): On theism, every possible world is, overall, axiologically unsurpassable (and this is due to God's existence, nature, or activity), whereas on naturalism, there are overall surpassable worlds.[30]

Evidently, this proposition supports GWMPST. But why would someone think that God's existence, nature, or activity ensures that all worlds in theistic modal space are unsurpassable?[31] With respect to God's *existence*, if God is the greatest possible being, it seems natural to suppose that the existence of such a being in a world renders it unsurpassable – and, of course, God is held to exist in *every* possible world.[32] With respect to God's *nature*, the defender of EWU could likewise argue that the existence of an unsurpassably *good* being renders every world it inhabits unsurpassable. This view could be considered an instance of the traditional idea that goodness is essentially self-diffusive.[33]

If the defender of EWU wishes to appeal to the value-adding effects of God's *actions*, things will be more complex, since, as noted, God's actions are thought to be contingent, whereas his existence is necessary and his nature is fixed. Now, on theism, God plays a unique and preeminent role in the actualization of whichever world is actual.[34] So the defender of EWU can argue that, from the vantage point of each world, God's actualization of it confers unsurpassable value on it. Now, God's actualization of a world is not one singular action. For example, God might create and sustain physical objects,

---

[30] Although not explicit in the formulation of EWU, I mean to preclude a scenario in which the worlds in theistic modal space are unsurpassed, but not very good. The idea, rather, is that all worlds in theistic modal space are supremely, superlatively good.

[31] I will not always repeat the modifier "overall," but it should be presumed.

[32] The underlying thought is that the overall axiological status of a world is significantly influenced by the value of its constituent elements. For relevant discussion, see Penner and Lougheed (2015) and Davison (2018).

[33] In his important discussion of Aquinas on creation, Norman Kretzmann refers to the following influential principle, which Aquinas often attributes to Dionysius: "Goodness is by its very nature diffusive of itself and (thereby) of being" (1990a, 217, and see also Kretzmann 1990b). This is one way to understand the axiological effect of God's goodness. (While I write here as though God's existence and nature are metaphysically distinct, this has of course been denied, most prominently by Aquinas himself.)

[34] This, of course, does not mean that God determines each and every feature of the resulting world. Consider, for example, random processes. If a world features such processes, God causes it to be the case that they occur, but he does not (by definition) determine their outcome. Next, consider libertarian freedom, which many theists think human beings exhibit. The actions of such creatures are (by definition) not under God's control, but they do affect how the relevant worlds unfold. On this view, God and these creatures *jointly* actualize a world.

God might frame the laws of nature governing them, God might intervene in the natural order, God might communicate with the denizens of a given world, God might become incarnate, and so forth. Everything that God does – and indeed, everything that God *refrains* from doing – ensures that the relevant world unfolds one way rather than another. All of this is included in God's *actualizing* a world. Accordingly, to assert that God's actualization of a world confers unsurpassable value on it is really just to say that the joint axiological effects of all these actions and refrainings confer unsurpassable value, in every world.

But is any of this really an *argument* for EWU on the basis of the axiological effects of divine activity? It might seem that it is really just a description of what a certain sort of pro-theist thinks, rather than a defense of it. The defender of EWU who wishes to appeal to the axiological effects of divine actions should devise an a priori argument to the effect that, *no matter* how God acts or refrains from acting, the overall effect will be immensely positive – indeed, sufficient to make the resulting world unsurpassable overall. Such an argument will presumably appeal to the divine attributes, along the following lines. As an omniscient being, God knows all there is to know about conferring unsurpassable value. As an omnipotent being, God will be able to bring about unsurpassable value. As a perfectly good being, God will be perfectly motivated to do so.[35]

I will not develop these pro-theistic considerations any further here; instead, I turn to a suite of objections.

Objections to EWU

Here are six objections to EWU, together with suggested replies. The first five allege, in various ways, that EWU is incoherent or implausible. The sixth specifically targets *theists* who endorse EWU.

(1) On theism, no world is overall unsurpassable.

This objection can be motivated by the thought that *only God* is axiologically unsurpassable. Now, to be sure, our definition of theism held that God is unsurpassable, not that God is *uniquely* unsurpassable. But it is nevertheless a fairly common expansion of theism that only God is axiologically unsurpassable. God sits *alone* atop the Great Chain of Being, so to speak.[36] If this view is

---

[35] These could be enhanced with specific proposals for how God will act in some or all worlds, and accounts of their positive axiological effects. But it's important to see that the modal space pro-theist is not required to devise an account of just what unsurpassable worlds look like; she simply needs to argue that theistic modal space contains *only* such worlds.

[36] The classic treatment of this concept is Lovejoy (1936).

correct, then it is a mistake to think that *any* possible world – let alone *all* of them! – can be *equal* in axiological status to God.

One reply concedes the point, and retreats to a more moderate defense of GWMSPT. Instead of insisting that God's existence, nature, or activity renders every possible world unsurpassable *tout court*, one could say that God's existence, nature, or activity renders every possible world unsurpassable *by any other world*, while holding that all worlds are surpassed by God. Another reply is nonconcessive: one could insist that on theism, God *and* all possible worlds are unsurpassable, while denying that this consequence is problematic for theism. Perhaps, for example, the underlying worry was that on this view, *worlds* would turn out to be worship-worthy, and that this would be theologically objectionable. But defenders of EWU can resist this consequence: they can hold that, on theism, although worlds are unsurpassable in value, just like God, nevertheless *only* God is worthy of worship, perhaps because of some other attributes (such as wisdom, justice, or mercy) that worlds evidently lack.

There is another way to motivate this objection: one could hold that every world is surpassed by another world, such that there is an infinite hierarchy of increasingly better worlds.[37] In fact, it is the dominant view in contemporary analytic philosophy of religion that, whether or not theism is true, every world is surpassed by another.[38] Authors who defend this view generally choose one (putative) good-making property of worlds, and then argue that it cannot be instantiated maximally. For example, Alvin Plantinga suggests that the *presence of people enjoying unalloyed bliss* is a good-making property of worlds, and then notes that for every such number of such people, there is a greater number (1974a: 34). On this basis he suggests that every world is surpassable. But this is too hasty. Plantinga offers no defense of the claim that it is *always* better for there to be more such people. Nor does he defend the tacit assumption that worlds that *lack* such people (or creatures at all) can always be improved.[39] Accordingly, it is an open question whether this way of motivating the objection can succeed.

A more abstract way to support the view that every world is surpassable by another invokes set theory. For example, Rubio (2020) points out that if the axiological status of a world is to be measured by the cardinality of its "locations of value," or the cardinality of the "intensity" of those locations, then no world

---

[37] Incidentally, this view is compatible with God's axiological status exceeding that of all worlds: worlds might *asymptotically* approach God's axiological status, after all.

[38] Notable defenders of this view include Plantinga (1974a: 61, 1974b: 168); Schlesinger (1977); Forrest (1981); Reichenbach (1982: 121–129); and Swinburne (2004: 114–145). But an important *a priori* argument for atheism, now called the *problem of no best world*, holds that theism is *impossible* if every world is surpassable. For discussion, see Rowe (2004) and Kraay (2010a).

[39] For discussion of these and other criticisms, see Kraal (2013).

can be unsurpassable, on the grounds that, as Georg Cantor showed, for every cardinality, whether finite or transfinite, there is a greater cardinality.[40] One response grants that cardinalities always be used to model axiological status, but insists that the mathematics outruns the metaphysics here: the cardinalities simply outstrip the levels of axiological status that there could be.[41] A different response denies that axiological status is in every case appropriately (or best) represented by cardinalities. Interestingly, Cantor himself seems to have held this view: he thought that God's goodness surpasses everything that can be measured by the finite and transfinite cardinalities. Indeed, he seemed to equate God with a level of value *beyond* all of these, which he called Absolute Infinity. Recently Mark Johnston (2019) has developed a Cantorian model according to which God's Absolute Infinite goodness confers Absolute Infinite goodness on every possible world.[42] Such a model, if plausible, can be used to defend EWU against this objection.

(2) On theism, it is false that all worlds are overall unsurpassable.

On EWU, *every* world in theistic modal space is axiologically unsurpassable. It follows that no world is better than or worse than any other – but of course this could be resisted by claiming that some worlds are indeed better than, or worse than, others. This, of course, is more modest than the foregoing objection, which held that *every* world is axiologically surpassable (either by God, or by infinitely many worlds, or both). Here are three ways to motivate this objection, together with some replies:

(a) One way begins with the conceivability of a small state of affairs than which there is a better (or worse) state of affairs, and then generalizes this to the judgment that some *world* can be bettered (or worsened).[43] For example, it is easy to conceive of one animal experiencing significant and preventable suffering for its entire life – and it seems obvious that such a state of affairs could be improved. Moreover, one might think, one can conceive of a world that includes only such animals, plus whatever is required for (and follows from) their existence. This seems to suggest that such a world is possible. And of course, such a world, like the initial state of affairs, seems eminently improvable.[44] But one could respond that this inference from conceivability

---

[40] Rubio's targets are Kraay (2010b) and Climenhaga (2018). Rubio does not claim to have shown that there is no best world; only that certain arguments to the contrary fail.

[41] Of course, a move like this must be well-motivated, not ad hoc. But, likewise, Rubio owes an argument for thinking that the metaphysics always corresponds to the mathematics here. (It's not clear to me who bears the burden of proof in this dispute.)

[42] Naylor (2020) also defends this view.

[43] Alternatively, one could appeal to brute intuitions about possibility.

[44] This method and example are due to Guleserian (1983).

to possibility isn't secure, particularly on theism. Thomas Morris makes this point:

> If there is a being who exists necessarily, and is necessarily omnipotent, omniscient, and good, then many states of affairs which otherwise would represent genuine possibilities, and which by all nontheistic tests of logic and semantics do represent possibilities, are strictly impossible in the strongest sense. In particular, *worlds containing certain sorts of disvalue or evil are metaphysically ruled out* by the nature of God, divinely precluded from the realm of real possibility (1987: 48, emphasis added).

In short, since conceivability is not generally thought to *entail* possibility, the defender of EWU can always say that the considerations favoring EWU above outweigh the probative force of the conceivability of surpassable worlds.

(b) A related way to support this objection appeals to intuitions about the axiological effects of *our* actions and omissions in the actual world. It seems obvious that the actions that individuals or groups can undertake, or refrain from undertaking, can make an overall axiological difference to the course of human history. For example, it seems undeniable that the actions that led to the near-eradication of slavery, the massive reduction in poverty, and the increased respect for the rights of persons in recent centuries have made the modern human condition better than it would otherwise be. And it is very tempting to suppose, further, that these actions have made the *actual world as a whole* better than it would otherwise be (whether or not theism is true). Likewise, it seems undeniable – not to mention tragic – that the individual and collective actions that resulted in environmental degradation, income inequality, genocide, and other forms of mass violence in the last few centuries have made the actual world *worse* than it would otherwise be (whether or not theism is true).

In response, it might be held that the axiological effects of our actions and omissions are simply too small, relative to the vastness of the actual world, for us to reasonably think that we can make an *overall* axiological difference to our world. This point can seem especially plausible when one keeps in mind that the truth of *theism* is at issue here. With respect to the putative overall *worse*-making effects of creaturely actions, one could respond that the goodness conferred by God's *existence* or *nature* will always swamp the relevant badness. Or one could say that God's *activity* will, in one fashion or another, outweigh the worse-making effects of creaturely actions, such that the resulting world remains unsurpassable after all. And, with respect to the putative overall *better*-making effects of creaturely actions, one could insist that it is more plausible to think that

God's existence, nature, or activity already confers unsurpassable value on a world, which, of course, cannot be bettered.

(c) A third way to support this objection alleges that there are *downsides* of God's existence that make some worlds in theistic modal space surpassable. These are *anti-theistic* considerations. The literature to date has focused on the putative downsides of God's existence for the lives of some or all persons. Anti-theists have held that on theism, relative to naturalism, persons have significantly (a) less freedom, (b) less dignity, and (c) less privacy; and, moreover, that (d) the world is less intelligible to persons, (e) commonsense morality is compromised, and that (f) some people's lives are rendered meaningless. I will consider these in Section 4. They could be harnessed, individually or jointly, to support the claim that at least some worlds are surpassable on theism.[45] But, of course, they are controversial, and I will also set out how critics have responded. Moreover, the overall probative force of these anti-theistic considerations pertaining to persons will need to be weighed against the probative force of *pro*-theistic considerations pertaining to persons. I will discuss six of these in Section 4 too.

(3) God cannot rationally choose a world to actualize on EWU.

Common expansions of bare theism hold that God's choice of a possible world to actualize is *rational, free*, and *worthy of thanks and praise*.[46] But these ideas seem to conflict with EWU. In this subsection, I consider the first of these ideas, and in the next two subsections, I consider the other two, respectively. On what basis can God rationally choose a world, given EWU? Clearly, God cannot base his choice on a world's axiological status – by hypothesis, they are all unsurpassable. Could God select a world at random? It's difficult to see how.[47] Could God act on a *preference* for one unsurpassable world over another? It's doubtful that this would be rational.[48] Following a cheeky suggestion due to Peter van

---

[45] These anti-theistic considerations are typically deployed to support the claim that some worlds or lives are better on *naturalism* than on theism. Here, however, they are deployed to show that some worlds in theistic modal space are surpassed by others in theistic modal space. Notice that these "downsides" all involve *persons*, so one could hold that such worlds are surpassed by some world(s) in which God exists but does not create persons.

[46] As I mentioned in Note 26, objections based on the idea that God confers special ontological status on one world cannot arise on the modal realism of David Lewis (1986). This pertains to objections (3), (4), and (5) in this subsection, and also to Section 2.3 (3) and Section 2.4 (2). Relatedly, objections (3), (4), and (5) presume that there is more than one world in theistic modal space.

[47] On this, see Kraay (2008a).

[48] Perhaps ordinary agents can be rational in acting on their nonrational preferences. But the idea here is different: it's just not clear how God could even have nonrational preferences in the first place. For a dissenting view, see Leftow (2017).

Inwagen (1988), perhaps God could simply issue the following degree: "Let some world be actual!" But this seems to place the mechanism of world-actualization outside of God's sovereignty, which may be at odds with theism.[49] A model will have to be devised according to which it can be rational for God to "just pick" a world, without relying on preferences, randomization, or "van Inwagenish decrees."[50] Whether this objection succeeds will, then, depend on whether such a model is plausible.

(4) God cannot freely choose a world to actualize on EWU.

God's choice of a world for actualization is widely held to be *free*. But it is controversial whether this can be so if every world is unsurpassable. Some philosophers hold that God can freely choose any one of the unsurpassable worlds (e.g., Flint 1983, Swinburne 2016: 126–149). But dissenters maintain that God's choice would be *arbitrary* or *insignificant* in such a scenario, and that this conflicts with genuine freedom (e.g., Fales 1994: 69; Wierenga 2002: 433). Defenders of EWU either need to block this sort objection, or else restrict their defense of EWU to models of God that allow God's choice of a world to be unfree.[51]

(5) The problem of thanks and praise.

If there are no surpassable worlds in theistic modal space, then it seems to make no sense to thank or praise God for selecting one of the unsurpassable ones "instead." Moreover, it's not clear that God can appropriately be thanked or praised for selecting any *particular* unsurpassable world in lieu of another.[52] In response, Senor (2008) concedes that on this view, perhaps God is not *morally* praiseworthy – but he urges that God is still properly praised *for who he is*, and properly thanked for *what he has done*. Bergmann and Cover (2006) and Daeley (2019) also suggest that God can properly be thanked even in the absence of divine freedom. Defenders of EWU will have to either endorse some such account of the propriety of thanks and praise, or else will have to give up the

---

[49] I'm grateful to Mike Almeida for suggesting this.

[50] For one such account, see Ullman-Margalit and Morganbesser (1977). For another, see Leftow (forthcoming).

[51] For more on such models, see Rowe and Kraay (forthcoming).

[52] Leibniz held this view:

> For to think that God acts in anything without having any reason for his willing, even if we overlook the fact that such action seems impossible, is an opinion that conforms little to God's glory. For example, let us suppose that God chooses between A and B, and that he takes A without any reason for preferring it to B. I say that this action on the part of God is at least not praiseworthy, for all praise ought to be founded on the reason which *ex hypothesi* is not present there. My opinion is that God does nothing for which he does not deserve to be glorified (1902: 6–7).

idea that, on theism, God is worthy of thanks and praise for his choice of a world.

(6) A problem for *theists* who endorse EWU: the actual world seems surpassable.

Theists, of course, think that God exists in the actual world. On EWU, God's existence, nature, or activity ensures that every world is axiologically unsurpassable, so theists who endorse EWU must maintain, *a fortiori*, that *the actual world* is axiologically unsurpassable too. This means that the actual world cannot have been better than it is. But clearly this Panglossian view can be resisted. For one thing, as mentioned in point (b) under objection 2.2 (2), it can seem very plausible to suppose that human actions and omissions, both individually and collectively, can improve (or have improved) the actual world. Moreover, theists who endorse EWU will have to reckon with entire families of arguments that allege, in various ways, that *God* could improve (or could have improved) the actual world in various ways. *Arguments from evil* hold that God could have and should have reduced or eliminated various tokens or types of evil.[53] *Arguments from nonbelief* hold that God could have and should have brought it about that more people have the explicit, conscious belief that God exists.[54] These arguments are standardly wielded against the claim that theism is *true*, but they can equally be directed against the theist who endorses EWU, precisely because they insist that the actual world is *surpassable*. A complete evaluation of such arguments is evidently beyond the scope of this Element, so I will simply record my view that the challenge they pose to theists who endorse EWU is formidable. (But of course, as we have seen, one needn't be a theist to endorse either EWU or GWMSPT.)

2.3 Second Argument for GWMSPT: On Theism, Every World Is Overall Good

EWU is an extremely ambitious view. Pro-theists who deem it too ambitious may prefer this more modest alternative:

> EVERY WORLD GOOD (EWG): On theism, worlds vary in overall axiological status, but every possible world is overall good (and this is due to God's existence, nature, or activity), whereas on naturalism, there are overall neutral worlds and overall bad worlds.

---

[53] A good introduction to the contemporary discussion is McBrayer and Howard-Snyder (2013).

[54] Important presentations of such arguments can be found in Schellenberg (1993, 2007, and 2015). For introductions to the voluminous relevant literature, see, Kraay (2013b) and Howard-Snyder and Green (2016).

Variants of EWG could be devised that set the threshold lower or higher.[55] Wherever it is set, the pro-theist bears the burden of showing that (a) the threshold itself is defensible, and that (b) it's reasonable to think that God's existence, nature, or activity ensures that *all* worlds in theistic modal space surpass it.[56] Pro-theistic considerations about God's existence, nature, and activity discussed in Section 2.2 could be harnessed to support (b), so I will not repeat them here. The first objection considered below challenges (a).

Objections

The six objections to EWU discussed in Section 2.2 can be retooled to target EWG, and I will briefly discuss each in turn. First, however, I discuss a new objection.

(1) No defensible axiological threshold.

EWG maintains that on theism, modal space includes all and only those worlds that are good overall. But is this model coherent? It is important to see that for it to be coherent, each world must be *good enough* to be compatible with theism. Let me explain. For simplicity, suppose that there are objective units of goodness and badness, and that a world is overall good just in case its units of goodness outnumber its units of badness. Granting this, it won't do to merely stipulate that the model of modal space expressed by EWG includes all (and only) such worlds. That's because what's envisioned is not just modal space, but *theistic* modal space, and at this point it is an open question whether it is coherent to suppose that God exists in a world in which the good *just barely* outweighs the bad. Perhaps God's standards are higher. This prompts an important question: just how high are the standards of an *unsurpassable* being?

Here we need to divide cases, and a dilemma will be revealed. Suppose, first, that there are unsurpassable worlds in theistic modal space as envisioned by EWG. If so, it is tempting to think that the only coherent threshold will be

---

[55] Alvin Plantinga, for example, defends a higher (but vague) threshold. He says that in theistic modal space,

> [A]ll possible worlds ... are very good. For God is unlimited in goodness and holiness, as well as in power and knowledge; these properties, furthermore, are essential to him; and this means, I believe, that God not only has [actualized] a world that is very good, but that there aren't any conditions under which he would have [actualized] a world that is less than very good ... The class of possible worlds God's love and goodness prevents him from actualizing is empty. All possible worlds, we might say, are eligible worlds: worlds that God's goodness, mercy, and love would permit him to actualize. (2004: 8)

[56] The higher the threshold, of course, the easier it will be to argue that some worlds (perhaps even the actual world) fail to surpass it. This thought can be wielded against theists who endorse EWG.

this: theistic modal space includes only unsurpassable worlds. After all, it seems plausible to suppose that only the *highest* axiological threshold is compatible with theism. But if so, then EWG is no longer a distinct scenario: it simply collapses into EWU. Next, suppose that there are no unsurpassable worlds, but rather an infinite hierarchy of increasingly better worlds. What is the overall worst such world in theistic modal space? It is tempting to think that for any threshold between possibility and impossibility that one might imagine, a higher – and better – threshold could be devised. But if so, *every* model of theistic modal space on EWG is surpassable, because the threshold could always have been higher, in which case *no* such model is compatible with the existence of an unsurpassable being. In short, on this horn of the dilemma, EWG is incoherent.[57]

Both horns presume that God cannot exist in a world that is overall surpassable. But this claim is controversial. I will examine it in Section 3.3 (4), but for now, I will simply note that critics have devised models according to which God can exist in surpassable worlds. If successful, these models can be applied in the present context to avoid both horns of this dilemma.

(2) On theism, either no world is overall good, or it's false that all worlds are overall good.

The first objection to EWU discussed in Section 2.2. held that *on theism, no world is unsurpassable*. The second held that *on theism, it is false that all worlds are unsurpassable*. Of course EWG is immune to these objections as stated, since it denies neither claim. But they can be retooled for the current context: the former becomes *on theism, no world is overall good*; the latter becomes *on theism, it's false that all worlds are overall good*.

The former holds that either *because of* or *in spite of* God's existence, nature, and activity, *every* world in theistic modal space fails to be overall good. No such argument has been given in the literature, and it's difficult to see how one might go.[58] The latter objection is more modest. It could be supported by adapting the arguments discussed in points (a), (b), and (c) under objection (2) in Section 2.2. The first relies on inferences from conceivability to possibility to show, in this case, that some worlds are not good. The second, adapted to this context, claims that examination of *our* actions and omissions reveals that the actual world fails to be overall good.

---

[57] Isomorphic reasoning motivates the *problem of no best world* (mentioned in Note 38) and also certain objections to the coherence of theistic multiverses. On the latter, see Kraay (2012) and Johnson (2014).

[58] Every anti-theistic argument in the literature to date focusses on the putative "downsides" of theism for persons. But of course not all worlds feature persons, and these arguments cannot apply to personless worlds.

The third, modified for this context, claims that consideration of the downsides of God's existence reveals that some worlds fail to be overall good. The responses to these arguments noted previously could likewise be adapted to this context.

(3) Worries about rationality, freedom, thanks, and praise.

Common expansions of theism hold that God's choice of a world for actualization is rational, free, and worthy of thanks and praise. In Section 2.2, I discussed objections to all three on EWU. Officially, they target a model of modal space according to which all worlds have the exact same axiological status, so, strictly speaking, they cannot apply here, since on EWG, modal space can include worlds that vary in axiological status, so long as they all meet or exceed the objective axiological threshold.

And yet, close variants of these objections *can* be leveled against EWG. To see how, let's consider three separate scenarios of what the modal space envisioned by EWG looks like. All worlds are overall good on EWG, but either (i) there is one unique unsurpassable world; or else (ii) there are multiple unsurpassable worlds; or else (iii) there is an infinite hierarchy of increasingly better worlds. On (i) and (ii), it might seem that God is not free to select a surpassable world. Likewise, on scenario (ii) it might seem that God's choice of any one of the *un*surpassable worlds in lieu of any other cannot be free or rational. Moreover, if God selects a surpassable world, on either (i) or (ii), this might be thought to count against God's rationality. Finally, as for scenario (iii), it can be urged that no choice of a world by God can be fully rational, since for any world God selects, God always has greater reason to select a better one.

I turn now to thanks and praise. Clearly, on EWG, God cannot sensibly be thanked or praised for choosing a good world *in lieu* of a nongood world, since *ex hypothesi* no such options are available. On scenarios (i) and (ii), if God selects an unsurpassable world, it could presumably be appropriate to thank and praise him for doing so in lieu of selecting a surpassable world. But on scenario (ii) it is not clear why God should be thanked or praised for selecting one unsurpassable world in lieu of another, and on scenario (iii) one might argue that no choice of a world is *fully* worthy of thanks and praise, since, for any world chosen by God, a better one could have been chosen instead.

Ultimately, defenders of EWG will need to endorse (or devise) some account of divine freedom, rationality, thankworthiness, and praiseworthiness that withstands these objections, or else restrict their pro-theism to models of God that do not involve these expansions.

(4) Problems for theists who endorse EWG?

I urged in Section 2.2 (6) that *arguments from evil* and *arguments from nonbelief* present serious difficulties for theists who endorse EWU. But it's far less clear that they present difficulties for theists who endorse EWG. That's because they typically do not allege that the actual world fails to be *good*; they typically allege (or at least entail) that the actual world is *surpassable*. Evidently, the claim that the actual world is *good* is rather more modest, and hence more plausible, than the claim that the actual world is *unsurpassable*.

2.4 Third Argument For GWMSPT: On Theism, Every World Is Overall Better

A pro-theist who thinks that EWU and EWG are too ambitious, or that one or more of the objections to them is decisive, could instead defend this more modest view:[59]

> EVERY WORLD BETTER (EWB): Every possible world is overall better on theism than it would be on naturalism, and this is due to God's existence, nature, or activity.[60]

Evidently, this view is compatible with theistic modal space containing surpassable worlds, and even worlds that are not overall good. Again, the pro-theistic considerations canvassed in Section 2.2 – arguments that appeal to the axiological effects of God's existence, nature, and actions, either individually or jointly – could be adapted to support EWB, and so I will not repeat them here.

Objections

The six objections to EWU discussed in Section 2.2. can be retooled to target EWB, and I will briefly discuss each one. First, however, I discuss a new objection.

---

[59] Here is Guy Kahane expressing this view: "On virtually any plausible understanding [of divine benevolence and goodness] God's intrinsic goodness by itself implies that a world would be made dramatically better simply in virtue of God's existence, even if that world was already very good" (2011: 675).

[60] This claim is not identical to GWMSPT. GWMSPT says that *modal space* is better on theism than on naturalism, but as I noted in Section 2.1 (g), this could be so without it being the case that *every* world is better on theism than on naturalism. Moreover, GWMSPT does not require that every world in theistic modal space has a counterpart in naturalistic modal space, but EWB does require this.

(1) No unique closest world.

It seems that that in order to assess EWB, one must compare the axiological status of each world on theism with the *unique closest* possible world in which naturalism is true. But perhaps there is no such thing. Here are four ways this could transpire: (a) perhaps two or more naturalistic worlds are equally – and hence unsurpassably – close to some theistic world; (b) perhaps no naturalistic world is closest to any given theistic world, since naturalistic worlds approach it *asymptotically* in degree of similarity; (c) perhaps the term "closest" is ambiguous between several different interpretations, none of which is the most suitable; and (d) finally, even if one clear sense of "closest" can be agreed upon, perhaps it is still *vague* which world is closest.

Here are two ways to reply. First, one could say that this is just a special instance of the problem of counterpossible comparisons discussed in Section 1.4. If so, then it is appropriate to hold that it is *epistemically possible* that there is a unique closest naturalistic world that is closest to each world in theistic modal space.[61] Another reply denies that a unique closest world is needed to ground the relevant comparison. Perhaps each theistic world can be compared to a *range* of naturalistic worlds in a way that can ground EWB. Of course, more details will be needed to flesh out this reply.

(2) Worries about rationality, freedom, thanks, and praise.

What about the objections that target divine rationality, freedom, and thanks and praise on EWB? These can be developed by dividing cases as we saw under objection (3) in Section 2.3. Ultimately, as before, defenders of EWB will need to endorse (or devise) some account of these attributes that withstands these objections, or else restrict their pro-theism to models of God that do not involve these attributes.

(3) Problems for theists who endorse EWB?

In Section 2.2 (6), I said that theists who defend EWU must hold, *a fortiori*, that the actual world is *unsurpassable*, and so they face serious challenges from arguments that deny this, including *arguments from evil* and *arguments from nonbelief*. In Section 2.3 (4) I noted that typical examples of these arguments do not count against theists who believe EWG. Theists who maintain EWB must hold (*a fortiori*) that the actual world is *better than it would be on naturalism*, due to God's existence, nature, or activity. This, of course, is compatible with the actual

---

[61] Of course, one might retort that one or more of these four scenarios can be recast as *challenging* the idea that this is epistemically possible.

world's being surpassable, and indeed with its failing to be overall good. And so it is immune to typical arguments from evil and nonbelief.

(4) No world is overall better on theism / some worlds fail to be overall better on theism.

Like EWG, EWB sidesteps the first two objections that were leveled against EWU. The former held that *on theism, no world is overall unsurpassable*, and the latter held that *on theism, it's false that every world is overall unsurpassable*. But of course EWB, just like EWG, denies neither claim. Nor is EWB vulnerable to the variants of these objections that were leveled against EWG: *on theism, no world is overall good* and *on theism, it's false that all worlds are overall good*. EWB, again, denies claim.[62]

But these objections can nevertheless be adapted to the present context, becoming *no world is overall better on theism than it is on naturalism, due to God's existence, nature, or activity*, and *some worlds fail to be overall better on theism than they are on naturalism, due to God's existence, nature, or activity*. The former is extremely ambitious, and it's difficult to see how an argument for it could proceed. The latter is more modest. It could be defended by appealing to the putative downsides of theism for persons. I will discuss these in Section 4. As noted earlier, they are controversial, and they need to be assessed together with the "upsides" of theism for persons that I will also discuss there.

2.5 Final Thoughts on GWMSPT

So far, I have examined three propositions that support *global wide modal space pro-theism* (GWMSPT): every world unsurpassable (EWU), every world good (EWG), and every world better (EWB), and I have considered objections to each.

GWMSPT is an ambitious and wide-ranging view. Those who think that objections to it are decisive, but who wish to remain global modal space pro-theists, have two options. First, they can argue that theistic modal space writ large is better than naturalistic modal space *in some respect(s)* due to God's existence, nature, or activity. This is global *narrow* modal space pro-theism. Second, instead of holding that God's existence, nature, or activity *ensures* that theistic modal space is better, either overall or in some respect(s), they could hold, more modestly, that this is *likely*.

And, of course, there are alternative axiological positions that one could take with respect to modal space writ large:

---

[62] EWB is also immune to the first objection leveled against EWG, which held that there is no defensible threshold that separates the good worlds from the bad.

GLOBAL MODAL SPACE ANTI-THEISM: Modal space is overall *worse* on theism than on naturalism, and this is due to God's existence, nature, or activity.

GLOBAL MODAL SPACE NEUTRALISM: Modal space is neither overall *better* nor overall *worse* on theism than on naturalism, as a result of God's existence, nature, or activity.

GLOBAL MODAL SPACE AGNOSTICISM: We should suspend judgment about what axiological difference God's existence, nature, or activity makes to modal space, relative to naturalism.

GLOBAL MODAL SPACE QUIETISM: The question of what axiological difference God's existence, nature, or activity makes to modal space, relative to naturalism, is in principle unanswerable.

Each of these axiological positions could be construed widely or narrowly, and probabilistic variants could be developed as well. Space does not permit examining these.

3 Actual World Pro-theism

In Section 2, I considered *modal space* pro-theism, which holds that modal space is better on theism than on naturalism. Here I examine a much more restricted version of pro-theism:

WIDE ACTUAL WORLD PRO-THEISM (WAWPT): The actual world is *overall* better on theism than on naturalism, and this is due to God's existence, nature, or activity.

Before discussing an argument for this view, I begin with some clarifications.

3.1 Clarifications

(a) It may be tempting to interpret WAWPT like this: "Consider the world that we in fact inhabit. This world is overall better on the hypothesis that theism is true than it is on the hypothesis that naturalism is true." But this is not what I mean. Instead, I mean this: "Whichever world is actual, given that theism is true, is overall better than whichever world is actual, given that naturalism is true." In theistic modal space, God's world-actualizing activity ensures that some world is actual. But in naturalistic modal space, some world is actual, and it is so without the world-actualizing activity of any divine being. What WAWPT claims is that the former is overall better than the latter. It does not, however, claim that either one of these worlds is the actual world that we in fact inhabit, nor that either one of these is similar to the actual world that we in fact inhabit, nor does it claim that these two worlds are identical to each other *but for God's existence and activity.*[63]

(b) This reveals that EWB (every world better), which I considered in Section 2.4, does not entail WAWPT.[64] EWB holds that every world is overall better on theism than it would be on naturalism. In other words, every world in theistic modal space is better than its closest comparator in naturalistic modal space. But as we have just seen, WAWPT makes a different claim altogether: it asserts that whichever world is actual, given that theism is true, is overall better than whichever world is actual, given that naturalism is true – without supposing that these worlds are each other's closest comparators.

(c) Modal space pro-theism is a comparative axiological judgment about two models of modal space. In contrast, actual world pro-theism is a comparative axiological claim about just two worlds: whichever world is actual on theism and whichever world is actual on naturalism. Actual world pro-theism is therefore more modest than modal space pro-theism.

(d) WAWPT assumes that there is something objectively special, something ontologically privileged, about the actual world relative to all others. This view is thus incompatible with the modal realism of David Lewis (1986), which denies that any world enjoys such status relative to all others.[65]

In Section 2, I considered three ways to support *global wide modal space pro-theism*: EWU (every world unsurpassable), EWG (every world good), and EWB (every world better). One might expect me to likewise consider three parallel defenses of *wide actual world pro-theism*:

ACTUAL WORLD UNSURPASSABLE (AWU): On theism, God's existence, nature, or activity ensures that the actual world is overall *unsurpassable*, but there is no equivalent guarantee on naturalism.

ACTUAL WORLD GOOD (AWG): On theism, God's existence, nature, or activity ensures that the actual world is overall *good*, but there is no equivalent guarantee on naturalism.

---

[63] Of course, *theists* who endorse WAWPT should believe that the world we inhabit is the former, and *naturalists* who endorse WAWPT should believe that it is the latter.

[64] If EWB were to entail WAWPT, there would be no reason to consider it separately.

[65] Clarifications (d)–(f) from Section 2.1 should be taken to apply here as well.

ACTUAL WORLD BETTER (AWB): On theism, God's existence, nature, or activity ensures that the actual world is overall *better than it would be* on naturalism.

But I will set aside AWG and AWB, and focus only on AWU, because neither AWG nor AWB entails WAWPT. AWG holds that whichever world is actual on theism is guaranteed to be overall good – but, of course, this does not establish that this world is overall *better* than whichever world is actual on naturalism. AWB states that the actual world is overall better on theism than *it* would be on naturalism. In other words, whichever world is actual on theism is better than its closest naturalistic comparator. But, as we have seen, the closest naturalistic comparator of whichever world is actual on theism may not be the actual world on naturalism, so AWB does not entail WAWPT.[66]

3.2 An Argument for WAWPT: On Theism, The Actual World is Overall Unsurpassable

Here is the ontological backdrop relevant to understanding AWU. On either theism or naturalism, exactly one world is actual. Theistic modal space and naturalistic modal space each contain a vast array of worlds that vary in axiological status. Suppose for a moment that in both, there is at least one unsurpassable world.[67] In theistic modal space, God's existence, nature, or activity ensures that the actual world is unsurpassable, but in naturalistic modal space, there is no equivalent axiological guarantee. I will first briefly set out some reasons why one might assert AWU. Then I will examine two reasons for resisting the claim that AWU entails WAWPT.

3.2.1 Supporting AWU

AWU states that in theistic modal space, God's existence, nature, or activity ensures that the actual world is unsurpassable. I will focus on God's activity. As we saw in Section 2.2, God's actions and refrainings in a given world ensure that the world unfolds one way rather than another. In particular, the defender of AWU holds that that these actions and refrainings ensure that, in theistic modal space, the actual world is unsurpassable. This idea is found throughout the history of philosophy. Particularly clear expressions of it are found in Plato's

---

[66] Here is a further reason for not considering AWG and AWB: they are entailments of EWG and EWB, respectively, and I discussed these views in Sections 2.3 and 2.4. I should also note, though, that AWG and ABW could be offered as considerations supporting a *narrow* version of actual world pro-theism.

[67] Of course, as we saw in Section 2.2 (1), this has been denied. I will return to this below in Section 3.3 (1). Also, I will not always repeat the modifier "overall," but it should be presumed.

Timaeus,[68] in Leibniz's *Theodicy*,[69] and in Kant's *Lectures on Philosophical Theology*.[70] It can be supported by an a priori argument that appeals to the divine attributes along the following lines. As an omniscient being, God knows all there is to know about conferring unsurpassable value on a world. As an omnipotent being, God is able to confer unsurpassable value on a world. As a perfectly good and rational being, God is perfectly motivated to do so. So, if there is just one unique set of actions and refrainings that God can undertake to ensure that a world is unsurpassable, God will undertake this set. And if there are multiple distinct sets of actions and refrainings that God can undertake to ensure that a world is unsurpassable, God will undertake one of them.[71] In contrast, on naturalism, God does not exist, and, moreover (as I have restricted the view) there are no other beings, processes, mechanisms, or forces that play anything like the good-ness-conferring role that pro-theists ascribe to God. Accordingly, there is no guarantee that the actual world in naturalistic modal space will be unsurpassable. This line of thought is enormously controversial, and reasons for resisting it will be canvassed in Section 3.3.

3.2.2 Does AWU Entail WAWPT?

Careful readers might wonder whether AWU really entails WAWPT. We have supposed that in naturalistic modal space, there is at least one unsurpassable world. Granting that there is nothing on naturalism that plays anything like the unsurpassability-guaranteeing role of God, perhaps it could nevertheless *just turn out* that the actual world in naturalistic modal space is unsurpassable. And in such a scenario, one might think, AWU would be true but WAWPT would be false, in which case the former does not entail the latter. This thought presupposes that whichever world is

---

[68] "God desired that all things should be good and nothing bad, so far as this was attainable. Wherefore also finding the whole visible sphere not at rest, but moving in an irregular and disorderly fashion, out of disorder he brought order, considering that this was in every way better than the other. Now the deeds of the best could never be or have been other than the fairest" (1980: 29E–30B).

[69] "Now this supreme wisdom, united to a goodness that is no less than infinite, cannot but have chosen the best. For as a lesser evil is a kind of good, even so a lesser good is a kind of evil if it stands in the way of a greater good; and there would be something to correct in the actions of God if it were possible to do better" (Leibniz 1986: 128).

[70] "That the world created by God is the *best* of all possible worlds, is clear for the following reason. If a better world than the one willed by God were possible, then a will better than the divine will would also have to be possible. For indisputably that will is better which chooses what is better. But if a better will is possible, then so is a being who could express this better will. And therefore this being would be more perfect and better than God. But this is a contradiction; for God is *omnitudo realitatis*" (Kant 1978: 137).

[71] The points expressed in Note 34 apply here as well.

actual on theism is axiologically equivalent to whichever world is actual on a naturalism, since they are both unsurpassable. But this is too hasty. To say that the former is unsurpassable is to say that no world in theistic modal space surpasses it, and to say that the latter is unsurpassable is to say that no world in naturalistic modal space surpasses it. The pro-theist can maintain that the former is nevertheless better than the latter, precisely because the former includes God's existence, nature, and activity, while the latter does not. If this is correct, this reason for thinking that AWU does not entail WAWPT fails.

Here is another reason for doubting that AWU entails WAWPT. We have supposed that there is at least one unsurpassable world in naturalistic modal space. But perhaps there is, instead, an infinite hierarchy of increasingly better worlds. And if so, someone might urge, perhaps some of these worlds are overall better than whichever world is actual on theism, even though this world is surpassed by no world in theistic modal space. If whichever world is actual on naturalism is such a world, then AWU is true but WAWPT is false. The best way for the pro-theist to reply is to hold that no matter how good worlds get in naturalistic modal space, whichever world is actual on theism will always be better, precisely because of God's existence, nature, or activity.[72]

3.3 Objections to AWU

Some of objections leveled against EWU discussed in Section 2.2. can be deployed against (or re-tooled to target) AWU. I will briefly discuss these, and I will then turn to a different objection to AWU that deserves more extended treatment.

---

[72] Both of these responses will be controversial. Those who think that the downsides of theism outweigh the upsides are unlikely to be persuaded. But, to date, all of the downsides of theism that have been proposed pertain to the lives of persons – and these responses do not presuppose that whichever world is actual on theism is a world that includes persons.

If these responses fail, pro-theists can concede that AWU does not entail WAWPT, and can instead defend more moderate versions of actual world pro-theism. For example, pro-theists can concede that it could *turn out* that, in naturalistic modal space, the actual world is unsurpassable, and indeed just as good as whichever world is actual on theism. But they could nevertheless point out that this would be an extraordinarily lucky accident: the odds of this transpiring on naturalism are *infinitesimal* (particularly in the absence of natural beings, processes, mechanisms, or forces that play goodness-conferring roles similar to God!) But in contrast, pro-theists could continue, on theism the actual world is *guaranteed* to be unsurpassable in virtue of God's activity. This thought could be developed into a *probabilistic* variant of WAWPT, or into a *narrow* version of actual world pro-theism.

(1) This conception of theistic modal space is implausible or incoherent.

The first objection to EWU discussed in Section 2.2 held that *on theism, no world is overall unsurpassable.*[73] This objection is evidently germane to AWU too. I discussed considerations for and against this objection in Section 2.2, so I will not repeat them here.

Another way to resist this conception of theistic modal space questions whether the *surpassable* worlds are genuine logical possibilities on this view. AWU asserts that on theism, God *ensures* that the actual world is unsurpassable. But "ensures" seems to suggest there is no possible scenario in theistic modal space in which a suboptimal world is actual – which is tantamount to saying that suboptimal worlds are logically *im*possible in theistic modal space. Critics can seize on this result, saying that it objectionably violates our strong modal intuitions to the contrary. Further, if the actual world is the *unique* unsurpassable world, and there are no surpassable worlds, then everything that actually exists, and every event that actually occurs, is *logically necessary* – and this also conflicts with very strong modal intuitions. This is the *problem of modal collapse.*[74] Here are three responses. One seeks to reduce the modal cost by positing that the actual world is a multiverse comprised of many universes, and using these universes to anchor familiar modal judgments.[75] A different response distinguishes between *possible* and *feasible* worlds: it insists that the surpassable worlds are logical possibilities, while also holding that they are *infeasible*: not actualizable by God.[76] A third response holds that surpassable worlds are indeed logical possibilities on theism, and, moreover, that God *could* actualize them. I will discuss this under objection (4).

(2) Worries about rationality, freedom, thanks, and praise.

Common expansions of theism hold that God's choice of a world for actualization is rational, free, and worthy of thanks and praise. In Section 2, I discussed concerns about these ideas that arise on each of three models: EWU, EWG, and EWB. These worries can arise on AWU as well. For details, refer to what I said about scenarios (i) and (ii) in Section 2.3 (3). Ultimately, those who hold that on theism, God's choice of a world should be deemed rational, free, and worthy of thanks and praise will need to develop or endorse some plausible account of these

---

[73] The second objection to EWU held that *on theism, it is false that all worlds are unsurpassable* – but this does not target AWU, so I set it aside.

[74] For discussion and references to other literature on this topic, see Kraay (2011).

[75] On this move, see Kraay (2011, 2012, 2015). For a criticism, see Almeida (2017a); for a rejoinder, see Kraay (2018b).

[76] This idea was introduced into the contemporary literature by Plantinga (1974a: 34–44, 1974b: 180–184).

attributes that withstands these objections, or else will have to excise them from their model of God.

(3) Problems for theists.

One need not be a theist in order to endorse AWU. But theists who endorse this view shoulder additional burdens. That's because they do not merely hold that if theism were true, then the actual world would be unsurpassable – they also hold that theism *really is* true, and that, accordingly, the world we inhabit *really is* unsurpassable. As noted in Section 2.2 (6), there are many arguments for the surpassability of the actual world. For one thing, it can seem very plausible to suppose that *human* actions and omissions, both individually and collectively, could improve (or could have improved) the actual world. Moreover, theists who endorse AWU will have to reckon with arguments that allege in various ways that *God* could improve (or could have improved) the actual world. These include *arguments from evil* and *arguments from nonbelief*. As I said earlier, a complete evaluation of such arguments is beyond the scope of this Element, so I will simply record my view that the challenge they pose to theists who endorse AWU is formidable.

As mentioned in point (c) under objection (2) in Section 2.2, anti-theists have posited various *downsides* of God's existence for persons and their lives. These could be harnessed, individually or jointly, to target *theists* who endorse AWU.[77] But, of course, they are controversial, and, in Section 4, I will set out how critics have responded. Moreover, the overall probative force of these anti-theistic considerations pertaining to persons will need to be assessed with reference to the probative force of *pro*-theistic considerations pertaining to persons that have also been advanced; I will discuss those in Section 4 too.

(4) God needn't choose an unsurpassable world.

The most direct way to challenge AWU holds that God needn't choose an unsurpassable world. Defenders of *satisficing* hold that it can be morally or rationally acceptable to choose the worse over the better. Some philosophers say that since satisficing is deemed acceptable in certain human choice situations, it should likewise be deemed acceptable in certain divine choice situations. An argument due to Robert Adams (1972) centrally involves such a move.[78] Adams considers the case of a man who decides to breed goldfish instead of more excellent beings such as cats or dogs. Adams suggests that the breeder satisfices

---

[77] This move targets theists in particular since the actual world evidently includes persons. In contrast, the nontheistic defender of AWU needn't hold that the actual world on theism includes persons.

[78] David Lewis (1993: note 16) was the first to refer to Adams's God as a satisficer.

by choosing a *good enough* species to breed, and says that there is nothing immoral or irrational in so doing, even if the breeder could have chosen a more excellent species instead (329). Adams thinks that God can likewise satisfice in choosing a world, by choosing a suboptimal one that is nevertheless *good enough*.

Adams even offers a particular model of what sort of a world would be good enough. He argues that God could defensibly actualize a suboptimal world with the following characteristics:

(a) none of the individual creatures in it would exist in the best of all possible worlds;[79]
(b) none of the creatures in it has a life which is so miserable on the whole that it would have been better for that creature if it had never existed; and
(c) every individual creature in the world is at least as happy on the whole as it would have been in any other possible world in which it could have existed.

Adams thinks it obvious that if God were to actualize a world with characteristics (a), (b), and (c), God would neither wrong anyone nor be less than perfectly kind to anyone, nor manifest a defect of character. These claims have not been well-received.[80] But even if they succeed, William Rowe has urged, they do not establish that God could defensibly select a suboptimal world:

> As forceful and persuasive as Adams's arguments are, I don't think they yield the conclusion that God's perfect goodness imposes no requirement on God to [actualize] the best world that he can ... What Adams's argument show, at best, is that God's moral perfection imposes no *moral obligation* on God to [actualize] the best world he can. His arguments establish, at best, that God need not be doing anything *morally wrong* in [actualizing] some other world than the best world. But this isn't quite the same thing as showing that God's perfect goodness does not render it necessary that he [actualize] the best world he can (1993: 228, and see 2004: 82).

Rowe holds that if God fails to actualize an unsurpassable world, then God's *action* in selecting a suboptimal world is surpassable.[81] And, he says, if God's *action* is surpassable, then *God* is surpassable (1993, 2004). Others have agreed, sometimes by suggesting that God's choosing the suboptimal over the optimal

---

[79] Adams assumes, merely for simplicity, that there is one unique best of all possible worlds. William Rowe, as we will see in the next quotation, follows him in this.

[80] For a discussion of criticisms in the literature, see Kraay (2008b).

[81] As I explained in Section 2.2, God's world-actualizing activity is the sum of God's actions and refrainings that, jointly, ensure that the world unfolds one way rather than another. To speak of God's *action* in choosing a world, or of God's *choice* of a world, is simply shorthand for all this.

indicates surpassability with respect to goodness, and sometimes by suggesting that indicates surpassability with respect to rationality.[82]

So, some philosophers think that God can satisfice by choosing a suboptimal world, while others demur. My sympathies are with the latter camp: I think it is far from clear that divine satisficing is plausible.[83] First, the analogical case for the propriety of *divine* satisficing begins with the propriety of *human* satisficing, but, in fact, it is rather controversial whether human satisficing in relevant cases is rationally or morally permissible.[84] Even idealized cases involving human agents are contested.[85] Second, even if arguments for human satisficing were uncontroversial, some of them rely on ideas that are inapplicable to the divine case.[86] And here is a third worry – one that extends Rowe's point quoted here. Satisficers think that in certain cases, choosing the suboptimal over the optimal is rationally or morally permissible. But just because an option is *permissible* does not mean it is *unsurpassable*. Consider supererogation. The satisficer says that rationality or morality requires one to choose at least a *good enough* option, but one can nevertheless insist that a supererogatory choice is rationally or morally *better*. If so, then a choice can be permissible while being surpassable. But it is plausible to expect God – an unsurpassable being – to make an unsurpassable choice, not a merely permissible one. If so, satisficing is not good enough for God.

In an important recent paper, Chris Tucker (2016) suggests that it could be morally and rationally acceptable for God to choose a suboptimal world, provided that God has an acceptable *countervailing consideration* that justifies his choice. (Tucker calls this *motivated submaximization* rather than *satisficing*, but the terminology needn't detain us here.) Tucker's idea is that God might have a special connection or relationship with certain people in a suboptimal world, and that this could constitute a countervailing

---

[82] See Flint (1983); Grover (1988, 2003, 2004); Quinn (1982); Wierenga (2002); Wielenberg (2004); and Sobel (2004).

[83] For details, see Kraay (2013a), which the remainder of this paragraph summarizes.

[84] It has been criticized in various ways by, for example, Byron (1998); Richardson (1994); Mulgan (2001); Sorensen (1994, 2006); and Bradley (2006).

[85] John Pollock (1983) imagines an oenophile's deliberating about when to consume a bottle of EverBetter wine, which improves with each passing day. Pollock thinks that the oenophile is rationally permitted to satisfice, by drinking the wine on any day when it is good enough. But Roy Sorensen, for example, demurs, stating that in this case, "reason declares there is no permissible alternative" (2006: 214, and see also his 1994). Dreier (2004) and Schmidtz (2004) would agree.

[86] For example, Michael Slote motivates satisficing by appeal to the virtue of *moderation*: one may turn down an afternoon snack or a second serving or dessert either because one feels no need for some additional good thing, or because one is perfectly satisfied as one is (1989: 10–20, 37–40). But such considerations surely do not apply to God's choice of a suboptimal world.

consideration. I disagree, for three reasons.[87] First, it's implausible to suppose that God could have a connection or relationship of the right sort. In the envisaged scenario, God deliberates, *in the moment logically prior to creating anything*, about which world to actualize. So there are not yet any actual people available with whom God can have a connection or relationship. But the special connection or relationship must nevertheless exist in the moment logically prior to God's choice of a world, since it is proffered as a *reason* for that very choice. The idea must be, then, that God has an *actual* connection or relationship with certain *possible* people. This strikes me as incoherent.

Here is my second reason for resisting Tucker's move. Even if we waive the foregoing worry and allow that God can have an actual connection or relationship with merely possible people, I do not see how such a connection or relationship could be *special* at all, still less sufficiently special to ground God's choice. Could some *causal* relationship make the relationship special? This seems doubtful, since no matter which creatures God chooses to create, God stands in the same causal relation to them: God is their ultimate creator and sustainer. Could it be that God *loves* some possible creatures more than others? This seems implausible, given God's goodness. Could it be that God just has a *brute preference* for some creatures? It's difficult to square this with divine rationality.

Finally, here is a more general worry for Tucker's strategy. Any attempt to devise a countervailing consideration that would justify God's choice of a suboptimal world must find a fine balance between two extremes. If it is insufficiently weighty, it will not justify the suboptimal choice. But if it is too weighty, the strategy risks incoherence by turning the putatively suboptimal world into an optimal one. (For example, consider Tucker's proposal that the countervailing consideration is the special connection or relationship that God has with certain people. If the connection or relationship is sufficiently valuable, the relevant world isn't suboptimal after all.) So, the countervailing considerations must neither be insufficiently weighty nor too weighty – they must be, like Goldilocks's choices, *just right*. I don't see how this can be done.

To sum up: while various attempts have been made to demonstrate that it can be rationally and morally acceptable for God to choose a suboptimal world, my view is that they face formidable obstacles, and that, accordingly, they do not provide an effective objection to AWU.

---

[87] For details, see Kraay (forthcoming), the final section of which I will now summarize.

3.4 Final Thoughts on WAWPT

This section has examined *wide actual world pro-theism*, which holds that whichever world is actual in theistic modal space is overall better than whichever world is actual in naturalistic modal space. In particular, I have considered one defense of this view (AWU), which holds that in theistic modal space, God ensures that the actual world is unsurpassable, whereas there is no equivalent guarantee on naturalism. I identified a range of objections to AWU, and suggested ways for pro-theists to respond to each.

Actual world pro-theists who are unpersuaded by these responses have several options. First, they can develop a different defense of WAWPT. Second, instead of defending *wide* actual world pro-theism, they can defend *narrow* actual world pro-theism, by arguing that God's existence, nature, or activity ensures that the actual world in theistic modal space is better than the actual world in naturalistic modal space *in some respect(s)*, rather than *overall*. Third, instead of arguing that God's existence, nature, or activity *ensures* that the former is better than the latter, whether overall or in some respect, pro-theists can hold – more modestly – that God's existence, nature, or activity *makes this likely*, either overall or in some respect.

And, of course, there are alternatives to all forms of actual world pro-theism:

ACTUAL WORLD ANTI-THEISM: The actual world is *worse* on theism than on naturalism, and this is due to God's existence, nature, or activity.

ACTUAL WORLD NEUTRALISM: The actual world on theism is neither overall *better* nor overall *worse* than the actual world on naturalism, as a result of God's existence, nature, or activity.

ACTUAL WORLD AGNOSTICISM: We should suspend judgment about what axiological difference God's existence, nature, or activity makes to the actual world, relative to naturalism.

ACTUAL WORLD QUIETISM: The question of what axiological difference God's existence, nature, or activity makes to the actual world (relative to naturalism) is, in principle, unanswerable.

Each of these axiological positions could be construed widely or narrowly, and probabilistic variants could be developed as well. Space does not permit examining these. Instead I will turn, in Section 4, to *local* versions of modal space pro-theism and anti-theism. As we will see, these are narrower in scope than the global views I considered in Section 2, but broader in scope than the positions considered here, which focus on the actual world.

4 Local Modal Space Pro-theism and Local Modal Space Anti-theism

In the previous two sections, I discussed *global wide modal* pro-theism and *wide actual world* pro-theism, respectively. In this section, I examine two views whose scope is narrower than the former, but wider than the latter:

> LOCAL MODAL SPACE PRO-THEISM (LMSPT): Worlds that are *relevantly and sufficiently similar to the actual world* are *better* on theism than on naturalism, and this is due to God's existence, nature, or activity.

> LOCAL MODAL SPACE ANTI-THEISM (LMSAT): Worlds that are *relevantly and sufficiently similar to the actual world* are *worse* on theism than on naturalism, and this is due to God's existence, nature, or activity.

Much of the literature on the axiology of theism involves considerations that bear on these views. In particular, the relevant worlds have been deemed better or worse in virtue of the axiological effects of God's existence, nature, or activity on *the lives of persons*.[88] For example, pro-theists have argued that persons can have meaningful lives only if theism is true, whereas anti-theists have argued that persons' lives are worse on theism because they lack privacy from God. Before examining these and other considerations, I begin with some clarifications.

4.1 Clarifications

(a) In order to analyze the axiological consequences of theism, one must first specify the value-bearing entity to be examined. The object of axiological scrutiny in this section is a *specific local region* of modal space.[89] Most pro- and anti-theistic considerations in the literature appeal to the axiological effects of theism on *persons or their lives*. Such persons are not, of course, found in *all* possible worlds. Nor are they found *only* in the actual world, since many nonactual worlds include such persons. So, as an initial approximation, we can say that the scope of the view is the local region of modal space comprised of worlds that contain persons.

---

[88] Here are three quick clarifications. By "persons," I of course mean *nondivine* persons. As for "lives," I include post-mortem segments of persons' lives, if such there be. Finally, while I here focus on persons, *non*-person-affecting considerations could also be offered to support these views.

[89] Just as "modal space" is a shorthand term for the entire ensemble of possible worlds, a "region" of modal space is a shorthand term for a proper subset of possible worlds. The views discussed in this section are compatible with accounts of possible worlds that treat them as concrete objects, abstract objects, and convenient fictions.

(b) This scope can be narrowed further, since the pro- and anti-theistic considerations to be discussed in this section pertain only to *persons like ourselves*. (There may be very different kinds of persons out there in modal space, but, at risk of sounding callous, they needn't concern us here.) So the worlds under consideration feature persons who are *relevantly* and *sufficiently* similar to us. While a complete defense of these views will require saying more about what makes a person relevantly and sufficiently similar to us, and, more generally, what makes a *world* relevantly and sufficiently similar to the actual world, we can make considerable headway without further specification.[90]

(c) Most of the pro- and anti-theistic considerations examined in this section pertain to *all* persons in *all* worlds in the local region of modal space. But one anti-theistic consideration pertains only to *some* persons – and I will examine it in Section 4.3.6.

(d) The pro-theistic considerations canvassed in Section 4.2 assert that certain goods can be obtained on theism but not on naturalism, while anti-theistic considerations discussed in Section 4.3. assert that certain goods are compromised or eliminated on theism, but not on naturalism.

(e) Individually, these pro- and anti-theistic considerations can be held to support *narrow* versions of LMSPT and LMSAT, respectively.[91] Whether these considerations ultimately support *wide* versions of LMSPT or LMSAT will depend, of course, on their *cumulative* probative force.

(f) One might worry that there is no sensible way to engage in axiological comparison of persons and their lives on the rival hypotheses of theism and naturalism. It might seem that doing so requires comparing the life of a person on theism with the life of that *very same* person on naturalism – and perhaps this comparison is impossible in principle. For example, it might be held that the person is *not just* a person, if God exists: she is a *creature, a reflection of God's image*, etc. – and, it might be insisted, this

---

[90] Three points are worth nothing. First, if this region of modal space lacks sharp boundaries, then the views in question can be narrowed to worlds that are *definitely* relevantly and sufficiently similar to the actual world. Second, note that LMSPT and LMSAT refer to the actual world – the world we in fact inhabit – whereas WAWPT does not, as I made clear in Section 3.1 (a). Third, if it is deemed too difficult to determine the contours of this local region of modal space, these judgments could be restricted to the actual world alone.

[91] Typically, it is held that the lives of persons are better (or worse) on theism than on naturalism, either in certain respects or overall. That the lives of some or all persons are better (or worse) is, of course, a respect in which the *worlds* they inhabit are better or worse. See Section 2.1 (e).

difference is significant enough to preclude the relevant sort of identity.[92] But we can set this worry aside. For one thing, it is just an instance of the general problem of counterpossible comparisons discussed in Section 1.4. Moreover, the views under consideration in this section needn't presume that this kind of trans-world identity is coherent. One could simply say that the persons in the local region of modal space are better off (or worse off) on theism than the persons who exist on naturalism, without presupposing that these are the *same* persons.

(g) Relatedly, one might worry that LMSPT and LMSAT presume – implausibly – that for every world in theistic modal space at issue, there is a *unique closest* naturalistic world. I discussed this worry in Section 2.4 (1), and set out two responses, so I will not repeat them here.

Section 4.2 discusses six pro-theistic considerations, and Section 4.3 discusses six anti-theistic considerations. Space does not permit a comprehensive discussion of each, so I will simply indicate their central features, mention key objections, and point to the most pertinent literature. Some of these invoke the axiological effects of *bare theism* as defined in Section 1.2; others involve common expansions of this view.

4.2 Pro-theistic Considerations

In this subsection, I discuss six pro-theistic considerations. Each holds that the relevant worlds are better on theism than on naturalism, and in a way that centrally involves the lives of persons. In particular, they hold that persons who inhabit the relevant theistic worlds have better lives than those who inhabit the relevant naturalistic worlds,[93] and that this is due to either to God's nature, or to God's activity, or to both. Theists who endorse them bear the additional burden of holding that the conditions they express are in fact satisfied in the actual world.

4.2.1 Ultimate Justice

Many people believe that on theism, God ensures that the wicked ultimately receive their just deserts, and that the good ultimately receive their due

---

[92] Slightly more technically: on this view, there is no trans-world identity for persons across the theism/naturalism divide. This does not preclude trans-world personal identity within theistic modal space, or within naturalistic modal space.

[93] One possible exception pertains to ultimate justice. In one sense, the wicked can be thought *worse off* in worlds where God ensures ultimate justice: they get their just deserts, so to speak. But of course it could still be held that the *worlds* in which God ensures this are better than their naturalistic comparators, even if some persons in them, in this sense, are worse off. (It could also be held that there is an important sense in which the wicked are *better* off for getting their just deserts.)

reward – and that there is no comparable guarantee of ultimate justice on naturalism.[94] This thought can been taken to support LMSPT.[95] Space permits neither a taxonomy nor an appraisal of the myriad ways that it has been, or could be, developed. Instead, I will outline three general constraints, which I will then apply to important versions of this idea that involve heaven and hell. First, for considerations about ultimate justice to be harnessed in favor of local modal pro-theism, they must be *theologically plausible*. By this I mean that (a) the idea that God dispenses such justice is a plausible expansion of bare theism; and that (b) the *way* God is held to do so is a plausible expansion of bare theism.[96] Second, the model must be *metaphysically plausible*. For example, if justice is dispensed *post-mortem*, as has often been held by theists, then a satisfactory model must be devised according to which *personal identity* is maintained after death. (Otherwise, it seems, the requirements of justice cannot be met.) Third, the model must be *axiologically plausible*: it must make it reasonable to think that the relevant worlds are *better* than they would be on naturalism.

One prominent family of views holds that on theism, God dispenses post-mortem justice by rewarding some people with an afterlife in heaven, while punishing others by consigning them to a post-mortem existence in hell. Many accounts of heaven and hell, and the conditions under which God would place persons there (and for how long), have been offered.[97] With respect to *theological* plausibility, a well-known objection holds that no amount of pre-mortem wickedness can justify certain degrees or durations of post-mortem punishment.[98] Such degrees or durations, the objection continues, are inconsistent with divine goodness. As for *metaphysical* plausibility, objections have been raised to heaven and hell themselves, and (as noted) to the idea that the conditions for personal identity are satisfied. As for *axiological* plausibility, one famous objection holds that immortality would ultimately be *tedious*.[99] This

---

[94] Tooley (2018) discusses this issue. Of course, it is logically possible that on naturalism, some being, process, mechanism, or force ensures that ultimate justice is dispensed. But as noted in Section 1.2, I set this aside. The same point applies to the considerations discussed in Sections 4.2.4 and 4.2.5.

[95] This view evidently assumes that persons are morally responsible, and that the rewards and punishments are dispensed by God are based on moral *(de)merit*. Both, of course, have been denied.

[96] Both (a) and (b) evidently require consistency with divine attributes.

[97] Some important analytic discussions of heaven and hell include Walls (1992, 2007) and Byerly and Silverman (2017). *Universalists* assert that everyone has a post-mortem existence in heaven, sooner or later. (See, for example, Talbott 2014). This has been offered as a standalone pro-theistic consideration (Mawson 2018).

[98] A parallel objection holds that no amount of pre-mortem moral goodness in creatures can merit the reward of heaven.

[99] Williams (1973). For a good discussion, see Hallett (2001) and Lougheed (2020b chapter 9, section 5.3). For a more general discussion of the advantages and disadvantages of immortality, see Nagasawa (forthcoming).

could be taken to mitigate, or even eliminate, the pro-theistic force of this consideration.

Interestingly, it has been argued that there are axiological downsides of *any* model according to which God dispenses post-mortem ultimate justice. Wielenberg (2005), for example, imagines a mother who voluntarily sacrifices her own life so that her child can live. Suppose that God will reward the mother after her death for her sacrifice – and that naturalism offers no such guarantee. Wielenberg thinks that examples like this show that acts of *true* self-sacrifice are possible on naturalism but not on theism. This thought can be held to reduce the pro-theistic force of ultimate divine justice, or it can be treated as a standalone anti-theistic consideration.[100]

4.2.2 Anchoring Morality

An aphorism widely attributed to one of Dostoyevsky's characters in *The Brothers Karamazov* states: "Without God, everything is permitted!"[101] The underlying sentiment, of course, is that morality is anchored in or by God. The history of moral philosophy is filled with many proposals from many traditions that seek to establish this claim in various ways. These are all expansions of bare theism, and are all controversial.

Divine command theories are particularly clear examples. These hold that moral obligations issue exclusively from divine commands. The most famous objection to such views is the Euthyphro Dilemma. In Plato's dialogue, *Euthyphro*, Socrates asks the titular character the following question: "Is the pious loved by the gods because it is pious, or is it pious because it is loved by the gods?" (1980: 10a, 1–3). Translated into terms germane to divine command theories, the question becomes: "If God commands some action, does (a) God command it *because it is morally right*, or (b) is it morally right *because God commands it*?" On (a), a worry arises for God's sovereignty, since the standards of rightness are independent of God. On (b), the worry is that moral obligations are arbitrary: the rightness of the command depends solely upon God's will, and God might have commanded otherwise.[102] In the contemporary analytic tradition, there have been several important efforts to defend divine command theories against these and other charges, including Quinn (1978), Adams, R. M. (1999), Wainwright (2005), Evans (2013), and

---

[100] For a survey of others who argue along these lines, and responses, see Metz (2019: 41). For further critical discussion, see Lougheed (2020b, chapter 5).

[101] For discussion of whether this sentence actually appears in the original Russian text of *The Brothers Karamazov*, see https://infidels.org/library/modern/andrei_volkov/dostoevsky.html.

[102] For a discussion that connects this point to the issue of counterpossible comparisons discussed in Section 1.4, see Davis and Franks (2015).

Hare (2015). But of course, these views remain controversial. For important criticisms of divine command theories, see Nielsen (1973), Wielenberg (2005), and Murphy (2011).

In order for God-centred moral systems to support local modal space pro-theism, it must be shown that (i) God really is needed to anchor morality, and that (ii) this anchoring makes the relevant worlds better on theism than on naturalism. To support (i), of course, one must vindicate a view, like a divine command theory, in which God plays such a pivotal role. This will ultimately involve not only assessing the (de)merits of various God-centred proposals on their own, but also a comparative analysis of such proposals relative to rival *non*-God-centred proposals. Evidently this will be an extremely complex matter. To support (ii), of course, plausible reasons must be given for thinking that God-anchored morality makes the relevant worlds better that they would be on naturalism.

4.2.3 Meaningful Lives

There is a robust literature on the meaning of life in contemporary analytic philosophy.[103] Much of it involves clarification, defense, and assessment of various proposals for (a) what "meaning" amounts to, and for (b) what conditions are necessary or sufficient for a life to be meaningful or to lack meaning. Again, alas, space does not permit a detailed survey. But an important fault line in the discussion of both (a) and (b) is worth noting: some proposals centrally involve a supernatural component, while others do not.

Thaddeus Metz, a leading scholar in this area, divides supernaturalist accounts into those that invoke a soul and those that invoke God (2019). I will focus on the latter. God-centred accounts of meaning typically hold that a person's life is meaningful to the extent that she freely fulfills (or at least attempts to fulfill) some divinely decreed *purposes* for her, which are themselves part of God's overall plan for the relevant world. If something along these lines is proffered as a necessary condition for meaning, the resultant pro-theistic suggestion is obvious: persons' lives can be meaningful *only if* God exists. More modestly, one could hold that this is not a necessary condition, but rather that fulfilling (or attempting to fulfill) God's purposes *enhances* the meaningfulness of a life in a way that is, obviously, unavailable on naturalism.

Of course, proposals like these are controversial. Specific objections have been leveled against the various accounts of God's purposes for people's lives. More generally, it has been held that it would be *degrading* or *dignity*

---

[103] Good introductions can be found in Seachris (2013); Mawson (2016); Metz (2019); and Seachris and Goetz (2020).

undermining for God to assign *any* purposes to people's lives.[104] Some critics agree that life-meaning centrally involves the (attempted) fulfillment of purposes, but deny that these purposes must be *God*-given. Perhaps they can be assigned, or generated, by other people, or groups of people, or the self, or the natural realm. Other critics deny that (attempted) purpose fulfillment is necessary for life-meaning, or that it enhances it.

Ultimately, the (de)merits of God-centered views of life-meaning must assessed relative to rival proposals. *Naturalist* accounts of life-meaning, as the name suggests, hold that life can be meaningful in various ways without any appeal to supernatural entities like God or souls. Some urge that there are objective requirements for naturalistic meaning; others insist that the requirements for life-meaning are subjective. *Nihilist* views about life-meaning hold that the conditions that would make a life meaningful, whether naturalistic or supernaturalistic, either cannot or do not obtain.

4.2.4 No Gratuitous Evil

Some philosophers have held that *if God exists, no evil occurs*.[105] Clearly, this thought could be harnessed to support local modal space pro-theism, since there is no equivalent guarantee on naturalism. But this is a minority view. It is far more commonly claimed that, on theism, God ensures that certain *types*, *amounts*, or *distributions* of evil do not occur. The most prominent example of such a view holds that, on theism, God ensures that no *gratuitous* evil occurs.[106] Let's say that an instance of suffering is *gratuitous* if neither its *occurrence*, nor God's *allowing* it to occur, is needed to bring about a greater good. Evidently, this consideration supports local modal space pro-theism, on the grounds that a divine guarantee that no evil is gratuitous will make the relevant worlds better than they would be on naturalism.[107]

Some very able philosophers have denied, however, that theism has this consequence. If their arguments succeed, this consideration cannot support pro-theism. I now briefly set out three such arguments and suggest criticisms.

---

[104] I will also discuss *loss of dignity* as a standalone anti-theistic consideration in Section 4.3.3. For a survey of the meaning of life literature on this point, see Metz (2013a).

[105] An important twentieth-century example is Mackie (1955).

[106] David O'Connor calls this the "Establishment Position" (1998: 72, 74); Jeff Jordan dubs it the "Standard Claim" (2003: 236). William Rowe has said that it "accords with basic moral principles ... shared by both theists and nontheists" (1979: 337). Stephen Wykstra has said that it is "a basic conceptual truth deserving assent by theists and nontheists alike" (1984: 76). Note, however, that there are some differences in how these authors understand the term "gratuitous evil."

[107] This consideration is thought to improve the lives of both persons and animals, but I here focus on the former. This consideration does not require that the evil experienced by persons or animals benefits those who experience it. I turn to such a stronger consideration in Section 4.2.5.

Michael Almeida (2020b) attempts to reduce to absurdity the claim that *if God exists, there is no gratuitous evil*. He derives a contradiction as follows. On theism, God is a necessary being, and so, given this view, gratuitous evil is impossible. However, Almeida thinks it obvious that at least some possible world contains gratuitous evil, whether or not theism is true. If so, it is *necessary* that gratuitous evil possibly exists.[108] But if it's necessarily true that gratuitous evil possibly exists, then God simply cannot eliminate it altogether, nor (hence) be expected to do so. The most promising way for the pro-theist to respond is to hold that it is illicit for Almeida to assert that *on theism*, gratuitous evil is possible, since that is the very point under dispute.[109]

While Almeida insists that, on theism, gratuitous evil is possible *simpliciter*, Peter van Inwagen and William Hasker think that gratuitous evil is possible *given* certain accounts of God's providential plans. Van Inwagen thinks the following story is epistemically possible: humanity has fallen into sin, and God's plan of atonement requires that human beings learn what it means to be separated from God, which, in turn, involves their experiencing significant tokens and types of evil. Now, van Inwagen continues, one might expect God to permit only the *minimum* amount of evil sufficient for God's purposes to occur – but, he claims, it turns out that there is *just no such thing* (2006). Accordingly, God has to permit an arbitrary amount of evil (within certain broad parameters), and, as a result, no matter how much God prevents, God could have prevented more, in which case some evil that occurs is gratuitous. One way to resist van Inwagen's argument denies that his story of fall and atonement is epistemically possible.[110] Another way points out that van Inwagen's argument tacitly appeals to the propriety of divine satisficing – and to argue, as I did in Section 3.3 (4), that satisficing is not good enough for God.[111]

William Hasker (1992, 2004, 2008) thinks that God must permit some gratuitous evil, since preventing all of it would compromise some important divine goals for creation. He says that God would want people (a) to come to know his nature, and (b) to place high priority on fulfilling moral obligations. But then, Hasker thinks, God's preventing all gratuitous evil would undermine moral motivation. That's because, given (a), people would come to learn God's policy of preventing all gratuitous evil. And then their motivation for (b) would be significantly compromised: after all, why refrain from causing or permitting

---

[108] It is a standard axiom of S5 modal logic that $\Diamond p \rightarrow \Box \Diamond p$.

[109] See my related discussion in Section 2.2 (2)a.

[110] Schellenberg (2007: 263–7) pursues this strategy.

[111] For more critical evaluation of van Inwagen's argument, and discussion of responses to it in the literature, see Kraay (2014).

evil when you are confident that God will ensure that any evil that occurs is nongratuitous? The most common response holds that people *can* believe that God prevents gratuitous evil without having their moral motivation undermined.[112]

Suppose, however, that Almeida, van Inwagen, or Hasker can show that God and gratuitous evil are indeed compossible – that would evidently block this pro-theistic consideration. But to concede that God can (or must) allow *some* gratuitous evil is not to concede that God can allow *any amount* of gratuitous evil. Pro-theists might say that on theism, God ensures that there is significantly *less* gratuitous evil in the relevant worlds than on naturalism. This is a more modest pro-theistic consideration.[113]

4.2.5 Involuntary, Undeserved Suffering Ultimately Benefits the Sufferer

Some suffering is undertaken voluntarily. (Consider athletic training). Some suffering is deserved. (Consider incarceration). But some suffering is neither voluntary nor deserved – and alas, it seems all too easy to think of examples. One might think that on theism, God prevents all *involuntary, undeserved* suffering. If this were true, it would be an important pro-theistic consideration. But many have resisted this claim.[114] Others have held, more modestly, that God would permit involuntary, undeserved suffering only if those experiencing the suffering *ultimately benefit from it.*[115] This view has come to be called *theodical individualism* (TI).[116] Two points about these benefits are crucial. First, they must be unobtainable without either the suffering actually experienced, or equivalent suffering. (Otherwise it would be natural to expect the benefit to be obtained in some other, less painful, way.) Second, they must be significant enough to outweigh the suffering in question. (Otherwise they won't be worth the price.) What makes this line of thought pro-theistic is the idea that God's existence furnishes a guarantee of this sort – whereas no such guarantee exists on naturalism.

An important criticism of this view is due to Jeffrey Jordan (2004). Echoing Hasker's argument discussed in Section 4.2.4, Jordan holds that if TI were consistently and widely believed, commonsense morality would be undermined, since there would no longer be any sensible reason to *alleviate* the relevant sort of

---

[112] For discussion of the relevant literature on this point, see Kraay (2019).

[113] I defend this claim in Kraay (2019); Hasker (2019) responds.

[114] Traditional responses hold that God's preventing *all* involuntary, undeserved suffering would unduly *compromise* creaturely free will, or the regularity or intelligibility of the laws of nature.

[115] Requirements in this vein are expressed in, for example, Tooley (1991); Rowe (1996); Adams, M.M. (1999); and Stump (1990, 2010).

[116] The term is due to Jordan (2004).

suffering, and, worse, there would be reason to *inflict it*.[117] Since Jordan thinks that commonsense morality is unimpeachable, he concludes that God isn't bound by TI. Gellman (2010), Lovering (2011), and Byerly (2018) all deny, in different ways, that TI undermines commonsense morality. Mawson (2011), meanwhile, offers a direct criticism of TI: he argues that it's implausible that morality requires human beings to permit involuntary, undeserved suffering *only if* those suffering benefit from it – and that likewise, no such requirement should be ascribed to God.[118]

If criticisms of TI succeed, pro-theists can retreat to more modest pro-theistic considerations in this vein. For example, Dustin Crummett (2017) adapts a suggestion from Marilyn Adams to craft the following requirement: "no suffering that God allows can leave its sufferer worse off than they could have been had God intervened to prevent the evil (or perhaps: if God generally intervened to prevent such evils)." Another more modest consideration holds that involuntary, undeserved suffering *more frequently* benefits the sufferer on theism than on naturalism. Defenses of such considerations will have to argue, of course, that they do not undermine commonsense morality in the way that their stronger counterparts are alleged to do.

4.2.6 Belief in God; Relationship with God

A bit of stage-setting is required here. *Arguments from nonbelief* hold that there is a tension between the idea that God is perfectly loving, on the one hand, and the idea that certain people fail to believe that God exists, on the other. The foremost defender of this type of argument is J. L. Schellenberg.[119] Schellenberg argues that God will seek a conscious, personal, meaningful, reciprocal relationship with all beings who are capable of entering into it and who are not resistant to it, since being in such a relationship will significantly enhance their well-being. In order to make such a relationship possible, Schellenberg argues, God will ensure that every such person believes that God exists. After all, he says, one cannot enter into such a relationship without believing that the other party exists. But, Schellenberg continues, many such people, both past and present, inculpably *fail* to believe that God exists – and, given the foregoing, this counts against God's existence. This reasoning can be spelled out in deductive, inductive, or abductive ways.

---

[117] As we will see in Section 4.3.5, this thought can be developed as a standalone anti-theistic consideration.

[118] For criticisms, see Maitzen (2010, 2013, and 2019).

[119] Important presentations of his arguments can be found in Schellenberg (1993, 2007, and 2015). For introductions to the voluminous literature on these arguments, Kraay (2013b) and Howard-Snyder and Green (2016).

Two pro-theistic considerations emerge. The first pertains to the benefits of (true) belief in God's existence. On theism, given this sort of reasoning, the relevant people come to believe what is, plausibly, the most important fact about the world they inhabit, about their existence, and so forth. On naturalism, however, there is no comparable guarantee that a comparable class of persons will come to learn the most important truth(s) about the world they inhabit, whatever they are.[120] What makes this consideration pro-theistic is the idea that, on theism, it is either intrinsically good or instrumentally beneficial for all such persons to believe that God exists.

The second pro-theistic consideration involves the axiological effects of *having a relationship* with God. Schellenberg himself suggests that having a relationship with God is itself intrinsically and instrumentally good (1993: 19ff). A pro-theist might say that, given Schellenbergian reasoning, the lives of persons in the relevant worlds are better than they would be, on naturalism, in virtue of the bare *possibility*, for all relevant persons, of having such a life-enriching relationship. Further, a pro-theist might say that on theism, at least some persons actually experience such a relationship, which also makes the relevant theistic worlds better than their naturalistic comparators.

Critics can, of course, object to these claims about the benefits of believing (truly) that God exists or of having a relationship with God. Critics can also object to the prior claim that God will ensure that all relationship-capable persons will, in fact, believe that God exists. Objections in this vein are normally offered in response to arguments from nonbelief that target theism, but they can also be deployed here. One common criticism holds that God might have good reasons to "hide" – namely, fail to ensure that some person at some time reasonably believes that God exists. For example, it has been said that God must sometimes hide to preserve morally significant human freedom,[121] or to make it possible for humans to come to believe in God on their own,[122] or to make possible a better relationship at a later time,[123] or even for the sake of justifying reasons that are beyond our ken.[124]

---

[120] Of course there could be justified belief in God on naturalism, but this is neither here nor there. The idea, rather, is this: whatever the most important facts about naturalistic worlds and the lives of their inhabitants are, naturalism furnishes no reason to think that all people capable of apprehending them will believe them. For a related discussion, see Davis (2014).

[121] See, for example, Murray (2002).

[122] See, for example, Swinburne (1998, 2004).

[123] See, for example, Howard-Snyder (1996).

[124] See, for example, McKim (2001). And for further discussion of the relationship between the literature on "divine hiddenness" and the axiology of theism, see Dumsday (2016); Lougheed (2018a, 2018b); and Hendricks and Lougheed (2019).

4.3 Anti-theistic Considerations

In this subsection, I discuss six anti-theistic considerations. Each holds that the relevant worlds are worse on theism than on naturalism in a way that centrally involves the lives of persons. In particular, they hold that persons who inhabit the relevant theistic worlds have worse lives than those who inhabit the relevant naturalistic worlds.[125] The first four hold that this is so because of God's nature, the fifth holds that this is so due to a combination of God's nature and activity, and the final one can be developed with reference to either God's nature or activity. Each one refers to a *loss* of some good: the core idea is that these goods are either *reduced* or *eliminated* on theism in ways that they are not on naturalism.

4.3.1 Loss of Freedom

God's omniscience is often taken to include infallible knowledge of the future. Suppose that God knows, right now, that you will finish reading this Element tomorrow. Since a proposition can be known only if it is *true*, then it is true, right now, that you will finish reading this Element tomorrow. But if it really is true, right now, that you will finish reading this Element tomorrow, then it seems that when tomorrow comes, you will lack the ability to refrain from finishing reading it – in which case, it is said, you are not free. The same reasoning applies to all propositions about future creaturely actions (both individually and collectively). And, of course, nothing in the argument turns on *this* particular moment's being the present. If, before there were any creatures at all, God infallibly foreknew exactly what they would do, then, given this sort of reasoning, no creature has ever acted freely.

Various responses have been proposed and debated, and here are some of the major ones. The first two deny that God has foreknowledge. Aristotle (in *De Interpretatione* IX) seems to have held that at a given time, propositions about the future are neither true nor false – they instead *become* true or false later, depending on how events turn out. On this view, there are simply no truths about the future for God to know, and so the problem dissolves. Second, some philosophers have held that, whether or not there are truths about the future, God does not *fore*know anything at all, since God is outside of time. A third response holds that persons have a certain sort of counterfactual power over God's past beliefs. Returning to our example, this response holds that if you refrain from finishing reading this Element tomorrow, you have exercised

---

[125] The first five hold that *all* persons in the relevant theistic worlds are worse off than the persons in the relevant naturalistic worlds; the last one holds that only *some* persons are.

the power to make it the case that God would not have believed today that you would finish it tomorrow. A fourth response denies that freedom requires the ability to do otherwise. This move is typically associated with *compatibilist* accounts of free will, but some *libertarians* have also denied it. A fifth response simply concedes that, given divine foreknowledge, creatures are not free.[126]

The fifth response can be harnessed to support anti-theism in the following way: the relevant theistic worlds are worse than their naturalistic comparators precisely because creatures are unfree in the former but free in the latter. How much support for anti-theism this provides evidently depends upon how great a good *the ability to do otherwise* is taken to be. Accordingly, one could resist this defense of anti-theism by denying that the absence of this ability is axiologically significant. Another way urges that creatures lack the ability to do otherwise on naturalism as well.[127] A third strategy, of course, is to endorse one of the other responses listed above, instead of accepting that divine fore-knowledge compromises creaturely freedom.

4.3.2 Loss of Privacy

An omniscient being would know everything there is to know – including everything there is to know about persons. God would know everything about our bodies, including their overall location, the position and movement of their parts, and everything to do with their health. Turning to the mental realm, God would know everything about what we believe and disbelieve, what we doubt, what we suspend judgment about, and likewise for every other propositional attitude or mental state. God would know exactly which inferences we make, and which we refrain from making. As Penner (2015) has pointed out, not only would God know what our conscious, occurrent beliefs, inferences (etc.) are, if we have subconscious or nonoccurrent beliefs, inferences (etc.), God would know exactly what they are too. Still further, Linda Zagzebski has argued that God would exhibit the attribute of *omnisubjectivity*: God would consciously grasp, with perfect accuracy and completeness, every conscious state of every human being (including every emotion felt) from that being's own unique perspective (2008, 2013, 2016).[128] These considerations generalize to all creatures and all times in the relevant theistic worlds.

---

[126] For a clear introduction to the literature on these responses, see Zagzebski (2017).

[127] This move could be made either while holding that the correct account of freedom requires the ability to otherwise, or while denying this.

[128] For an extended discussion of omnisubjectivity in the context of anti-theism, see Lougheed (2020b, chapter 3, section 8).

It has been suggested that God's knowledge of creatures supports anti-theism.[129] One way to develop this thought says that, necessarily, God objectionably violates at least some people's (perhaps *all* people's) *right to privacy*. A full development of this line of thinking requires an account of what the right to privacy is and how God violates it. But these considerations can be pressed in favor of anti-theism without holding that God violates a *right* to privacy: one can simply urge that in the relevant theistic worlds, creaturely privacy is compromised in a way that it is not in the relevant naturalistic worlds, and that this makes the former worse than the latter.[130]

For example, it could be urged that it is intrinsically bad for God to have such complete knowledge of creatures' minds and bodies. Alternatively, it could be urged that this is instrumentally bad. In the latter vein, it has been argued that God's knowledge of creatures would (a) undermine the point of prayer; (b) inhibit the ability of creatures to develop their autonomy or character (or, more generally, to flourish); and that it would (c) inhibit creatures' ability to develop trust in, or intimacy with, God.

A minority response to this anti-theistic consideration urges that God would lack the relevant knowledge.[131] But it is more commonly held that it is neither intrinsically nor instrumentally *bad* for God to have this knowledge, or even that this is either intrinsically or instrumentally *good*. With respect to the latter, it has been held that God's knowledge of creatures is a precondition (a) for loving them; (b) for having relationships with them; (c) for acting providentially and dispensing justice; and also that (d) creatures' awareness of the scope of God's knowledge has morally salutary effects.[132] A complete assessment of the axiological import of God's knowledge of creatures will, of course, involve assessing the probative force of these considerations, both individually and jointly.

4.3.3 Loss of Dignity

Guy Kahane mentions a cluster of considerations that, following Lougheed (2020b, chapter 4), I will group together under *loss of dignity*. Kahane points to the "hierarchical character" of theistic worlds, noting that on theism, human beings "necessarily occupy a subordinate position in relation to a being that is

---

[129] Kahane (2011, 2018); Lougheed (2020b, chapter 3).

[130] This, of course, need not presume that *perfect* privacy is possible on naturalism.

[131] See, for example, Tooley (2018).

[132] For discussion God and privacy, see Lackey (1985); Falls-Corbitt and McLain (1992); Davison (1997); Taliaferro (1989); Penner (2015); Penner and Lougheed (2015); Elliot and Soifer (2017); Hall (2020); and Lougheed (2020b, chapter 3).

vastly superior … in every respect" (2018: 110). This, in his view, involves several considerations: (a) humans are *causally* subordinate, since their existence depends upon God's creating and sustaining activity and hence they (b) owe God a debt for their very existence; (c) humans have been created (individually and corporately) for God's purposes;[133] and (d) their moral status is vastly lower than God's; (e) humans are utterly insignificant in the cosmic scheme of things; and (f) they remain forever in a child-like state relative to God (110–116).[134] Kahane thinks that these considerations are significant: "[t]he hierarchical character of a Godly world is its most fundamental fact, the fact around which life must revolve. There is nothing remotely comparable in the naturalist world" (114). Considerations like these can be taken to support local modal space anti-theism, on the grounds that (a)–(f) are respects in which the persons like ourselves have less dignity on theism than on naturalism.

Considerations (a)–(f) are important, but are so far underdeveloped in the literature. More work needs to be done to flesh out what is meant by "dignity" in this context, and exactly how considerations like these undermine it. But here are some brief suggestions for how critics might reply. One could object that (a) and (b) do not show that persons have less dignity on theism than on naturalism. After all, persons *depend upon* other persons for their existence, and *owe* other persons in various ways and at various times, but this is not generally thought to reduce our dignity. With respect to (c), one could deny that divinely conferred purposes are dignity compromising, particularly if fulfilling, or attempting to fulfill them, is necessary for one's life to be meaningful.[135] Consideration (d) evidently requires that one's moral status tracks one's dignity, but this could be resisted. Consideration (e) can be resisted on the grounds that being created and known (and, perhaps especially, being *loved*) by God *confers*, rather than eliminates, "cosmic significance."[136] Finally, as Kahane acknowledges, many

---

[133] In Section 4.2.3, we saw that some think that human lives require divinely assigned *purposes* in order to be meaningful – and I mentioned the objection that being assigned a purpose by God is degrading: *dignity-reducing or dignity-destroying*. This point about purposes can be detached from life-meaning. Perhaps, on theism, God assigns us purposes (individually or collectively), and it's *not* the case that either fulfilling them, or attempting to, is necessary for life-meaning, but nevertheless it *is* the case that being assigned them is dignity reducing or dignity destroying.

[134] Kahane includes *loss of privacy* in this cluster of anti-theistic considerations. Following Lougheed (2020b), I have treated it separately because there is a larger literature that concerns it.

[135] Lougheed (2020b, chapter 4) notes that many theists believe that an important purpose God assigns to persons is to *pursue a relationship with God*, and he endorses a principle articulated by Metz (2013b: 103) to the effect that it is *disrespectful* to create any person for any purpose other than to pursue its own purposes. But, as we saw in Section 4.2.6, it is often held that having a relationship with God significantly *enhances* our well-being, and it's not clear that being assigned *such* a purpose is automatically dignity compromising, particularly if (as most theists hold) one is free to reject this relationship.

[136] But see Kahane (2014).

theists find nothing troubling about (f) whatsoever – indeed, many derive great comfort from it – so, at least, the axiological intuitions driving it are controversial (2018: 112).

4.3.4 Loss of Knowledge or Understanding

Kahane speculates *en passant* that in theistic worlds, "it would be pointless for us to strive for a complete and unqualified understanding of the universe" (2011: 681–2, and see also his 2018, 110). More recently, Stephen Maitzen (2018) has developed an anti-theistic argument in this vein.[137] He begins by drawing what he takes to be the definitive distinction between naturalism and theism. He states that on naturalism, "*purposes aren't fundamental*: every being, action, or whatever, that has a purpose (a goal, a *telos*) arises from things that have no purpose" (138). In contrast, "theism regards God's intentions as *fundamental* to the universe" (141). He thinks that, given this distinction, on theism "we can't hope to understand the universe as deeply as we might want by means of our most reliable (i.e., natural-scientific) methods", whereas on naturalism, "human discovery [can be] limitless in depth" (139).

Let's grant Maitzen that, *ceteris paribus*, theistic worlds feature more teleological explanations than naturalistic worlds, and that these explanations simply cannot be uncovered using the tools of science. For his argument to succeed, it must be the case that (a) creaturely knowledge or understanding is thereby more circumscribed in theistic worlds, at least in some respects, and that (b) this makes them *worse* than their naturalistic comparators.[138] With respect to (a), as Maitzen concedes, pro-theists can hold that all the scientific understanding that is possible on naturalism is also possible on theism.[139] On theism, however, there is an *additional* object of possible knowledge or understanding: God. Now, even if Maitzen is right that *science* can furnish no knowledge or understanding about God whatsoever, it may nevertheless be that, on theism, *philosophical* or *theological* arguments can deliver significant knowledge or understanding of God – even if, let's suppose, it will always be incomplete. Moreover, such arguments may well furnish knowledge or understanding regarding other important matters. For example, some such arguments purport to show that certain phenomena are better explained on theism than on naturalism. Fine-tuning arguments hold that theism better explains why the universe is biophilic

---

[137] See also Lougheed (2020b, chapter 5).

[138] Anti-theistic arguments in this vein needn't suggest, of course, that complete or unlimited knowledge or understanding is possible on naturalism.

[139] Lougheed (2020b, chapter 5) rightly cautions that this is so only if God does not intervene in the natural order excessively.

(life-permitting); cosmological arguments claim that theism better explains why the universe exists; and the evolutionary argument against naturalism holds that theism better explains the reliability of our cognitive faculties.[140] Of course, arguments like these are enormously controversial. But if any of them succeed, they can be harnessed to block Maitzen's conclusion. Finally, theistic worlds contain an additional mechanism for conferring knowledge and understanding that naturalistic worlds evidently lack: *divine revelation*.[141]

Turning to (b), critics could reply that even if the possibilities for knowledge or understanding are more circumscribed in theistic worlds, it's not clear that this makes them worse than their comparators. After all, perhaps these limits on knowledge or understanding have salutary effects, such as reducing epistemic hubris, or making possible certain valuable experiences of mystery, or making possible certain goods involved in individual and cooperative investigation into God's existence, nature, and activity.[142]

4.3.5 Loss of the Intelligibility of Commonsense Morality

As we saw in Section 4.2.2, some pro-theists have held that only God can anchor morality. Anti-theists can argue, on the contrary, that theism reduces or eliminates the intelligibility of commonsense morality. Consider, for example, the idea introduced in Section 4.2.5: *theodical individualism* (TI). This holds that on theism, God ensures that those who experience involuntary, undeserved suffering *ultimately benefit* from it. While this is a pro-theistic consideration, it can also be harnessed in service of anti-theism.[143] As we saw, Jeff Jordan (2004) argues that TI corrupts commonsense morality, since, on this view, there is no longer any sensible reason to *alleviate* the relevant sort of suffering, and, moreover, there is reason to *inflict it*.[144] Jordan thinks that since commonsense morality requires us to minimize or prevent this sort of suffering, theists should reject TI. In an important paper, Stephen Maitzen (2009) argues that since TI and commonsense morality are both highly plausible, *theism* should be rejected.[145] Anti-theists, meanwhile, can argue

---

[140] On fine-tuning arguments, see Manson (2003); on cosmological arguments, see Almeida (2018); and on the evolutionary argument against naturalism, see Beilby (2002). For a more general discussion of the explanatory (de)merits of theism, see Rasmussen and Leon (2019).

[141] For criticisms of Maitzen in a similar vein, see Crummett (2019).

[142] The latter are invoked by Swinburne (1998, 210–212) in his response to Schellenberg (1993).

[143] This needn't be paradoxical: it could be that TI makes the relevant worlds better in some respects, and worse in others.

[144] Crummett (2017) argues that principles similar to TI that are endorsed by Eleonore Stump and Marilyn Adams also subvert commonsense morality – as well as having other deleterious effects.

[145] For discussion, see Gellman (2010); Mawson (2011); Lovering (2011); Byerly (2018); and Maitzen (2010, 2013, and 2019).

that if TI is a plausible expansion of bare theism, then the resultant reduction or elimination of the intelligibility of morality is an anti-theistic consequence.[146] As we saw in Section 4.2.5, there are two basic ways for pro-theists to reply: they can either deny that TI is a plausible expansion of theism, or they can deny that TI reduces or eliminates the intelligibility of commonsense morality.

4.3.6 Loss of Meaning

In Section 4.2.3, I discussed the pro-theistic idea that God's existence, nature, or activity is either *necessary* for, or *enhances*, the meaningfulness of crea-turely lives. In contrast, anti-theists can argue that theism *reduces* or *elimin-ates* the meaningfulness of at least some creaturely lives. Here is the basic idea. Some people are deeply committed to pursuing or attaining certain goods, to the point that the (rational) pursuit, or the attainment, of these goods is essential for their lives to be meaningful. But suppose that theism inhibits the attainment of these goods, or renders their pursuit irrational, in ways that naturalism does not. If so, the prospects for meaning in such persons' lives are curtailed or eliminated on theism relative to naturalism. In principle, this argument could be fleshed out with any of the anti-theistic considerations canvassed so far.[147] Consider, for example, privacy. Suppose that someone is so invested in pursuing or attaining privacy that so doing is essential for her life to be meaningful. An anti-theist might hold that theism inhibits the attainment of complete privacy, and renders its pursuit irrational, in a way that naturalism does not – and that, accordingly, the meaningfulness of such a person's life on theism is reduced or eliminated.

Notice that even if this argument succeeds, its scope is extremely limited: it applies only to persons who are very, very deeply – and reasonably – committed to pursuing or attaining the relevant good(s).[148] Moreover, here are three objections. First, one could deny that theism entails the reduction or elimination

---

[146] Here are three related anti-theistic considerations. First, one could argue that if TI were widely and reasonably believed, this would undermine our moral motivation. (On this, see Hasker 1992.) Second, Wielenberg (2018) argues that those who accept both TI and the Christian injunction *to love our neighbors as ourselves* will experience negative psychological conse-quences that will make it impossible for them to be happy, and render their lives absurd. (For criticisms, see Crummett 2019.) Third, one could argue that morally wrong actions are, in an important sense, *worse* on theism than on naturalism: that's because on theism, they are also *sins* – offences against God – which makes them worse than they would otherwise be.

[147] Kahane (2011) first introduced an argument along these lines, to which he appears highly sympathetic. For discussion, see Kraay and Dragos (2013); Penner (2015); Lougheed (2017); Penner (2018); and Lougheed (2020b, chapter 2).

[148] Lougheed (2020b, chapter 3) discusses the fictional case of Sally, who requires privacy for her life to be meaningful.

of the relevant goods in the first place. Second, one could deny that the meaningfulness of any person's life ever depends to such a great extent upon the attainment or rational pursuit of the goods canvassed in Sections 4.3.1–4.3.5. Third, one could hold that even if theism renders the complete *attainment* of these goods impossible, it does not automatically render *pursuing them* irrational. Suppose, for example, that in theistic worlds there are persons who rationally fail to believe (truly) that God exists.[149] Such persons could be perfectly rational in pursuing these goods, since they have no reason to think that God exists and makes them unattainable.[150]

4.4 Final Thoughts on LMSPT and LMSAT

The six pro-theistic considerations discussed in Section 4.2. can be deployed to support local modal space pro-theism (LMSPT), while the six anti-theistic considerations discussed in Section 4.3 can be harnessed in favor of local modal space anti-theism (LMSAT). Individually, these pro- and anti-theistic considerations can be held to support *narrow* versions of LMSPT and LMSAT, respectively. As noted in Section 4.1 (e), whether these considerations ultimately support *wide* versions of these views will depend on their *cumulative* probative force.

Assessing this thoroughly will be an extremely complex matter, which space does not permit. But one point about the interplay between these considerations is worth mentioning. Section 4.2.4 examined the idea that in theistic worlds, there is no gratuitous evil, and Section 4.2.5 examined the idea that in theistic worlds, involuntary, undeserved suffering ultimately benefits the sufferer. Both are controversial – but suppose that they are plausible. If so, they mitigate the import of the anti-theistic considerations canvassed in Section 4.3 in the following ways: (a) to the extent that these "downsides" of theism constitute or bring about *evil*, theism provides a guarantee that no such evil will be gratuitous; and (b) to the extent that these "downsides" of theism constitute or cause *suffering*, this suffering will ultimately benefit the sufferer.[151]

Assessment of the individual and cumulative probative force of the twelve considerations discussed in Sections 4.2 and 4.3 might lead one to endorse narrow or wide LMSPT or LMSAT.[152] More modest versions of both are also available: instead of holding that God's existence, nature, or activity *ensures*

---

[149] Kahane (2011: 692–693) mentions this move briefly.

[150] The anti-theist could retort that lives thoroughly structured around pursuing an unattainable goal are *absurd*, even if it is not irrational to pursue them. For more discussion, see Kraay and Dragos (2013).

[151] For critical discussion of (a), see Kahane (forthcoming).

[152] If the argument for local wide anti-theism succeeds, it also defeats the pro-theistic view EWB (every world better) discussed in Section 2.4.

that the relevant worlds are better (or worse) than their comparators, one could hold that God's existence, nature, or activity *makes it likely* that the relevant worlds are better (or worse) than their comparators, either in certain respects or overall.

And, of course, three other views are available, and each could be construed either widely or narrowly, and as involving either certainties or likelihoods:

> LOCAL MODAL SPACE NEUTRALISM: Worlds that are relevantly and sufficiently similar to the actual world are neither better nor worse on theism than on naturalism due to God's existence, nature, or activity.

> LOCAL MODAL SPACE AGNOSTICISM: We should suspend judgment about what axiological difference God's existence, nature, or activity makes to worlds that are relevantly and sufficiently similar to the actual world, relative to naturalism.

> LOCAL MODAL SPACE QUIETISM: The question of what axiological difference God's existence, nature, or activity makes to worlds that are relevantly and sufficiently similar to the actual world (relative to naturalism) is, in principle, unanswerable.

References

Adams, M. M. (1999) *Horrendous Evils and the Goodness of God.* Ithaca, NY: Cornell University Press.

Adams, R. M. (1972) Must God create the best? *The Philosophical Review* **81**: 317–332.

Adams, R. M. (1999) *Finite and Infinite Goods*. New York: Oxford University Press.

Almeida, M. (2017a) The Multiverse and divine creation. *Religions* **8**: 1–10.

Almeida, M. (2017b) Theistic modal realism I: the challenge of theistic actualism. *Philosophy Compass* **12**: 1–14.

Almeida, M. (2017c) Theistic modal realism II: theoretical benefits. *Philosophy Compass* **12**: 1–17.

Almeida, M. (2018) *Cosmological Arguments*. Cambridge: Cambridge University Press.

Almeida, M. (2020a) On discovering God in the pluriverse. In K. Lougheed, *ed., Four Views on the Axiology of Theism*. London: Bloomsbury, pp. 19–40.

Almeida, M. (2020b) On necessary gratuitous evils. *European Journal for Philosophy of Religion*.

Beilby, J. (2002) *Naturalism Defeated? Essays on Plantinga's Evolutionary Argument against Naturalism*. Ithaca, NY: Cornell University Press.

Bergmann, M. and Cover, J. A. (2006) Divine responsibility without divine freedom. *Faith and Philosophy* **23**: 381–408.

Beshears, K. (2019) Athens without a statue to the unknown God. *Themelios* **44**: 517–529.

Bradley, B. (2006) Against satisficing consequentialism. *Utilitas* **18**: 97–108.

Buckareff, A. and Nagasawa, Y., *eds.* (2016) *Alternative Concepts of God: Essays on the Metaphysics of the Divine*. Oxford: Oxford University Press.

Byerly, T. R. (2018) Ordinary morality does not imply atheism. *International Journal for Philosophy of Religion* **83**: 85–96.

Byerly, T. R. and Silverman, E., *eds.* (2017) *Paradise Understood: New Philosophical Essays about Heaven*. Oxford: Oxford University Press.

Byron, M. (1998) Satisficing and optimality. *Ethics* **109**: 67–93.

Chang, R. (1997) *Incommensurability, Incomparability, and Practical Reason*. Cambridge, MA: Harvard University Press.

Citron, G. (*ms.*) Theapathy and theaffectivity: on (not) caring about God. www.academia.edu/26321811/Theapathy_and_Theaffectivity_On_Not_Caring_About_God.

Climenhaga, N. (2018) Infinite value and the best of all possible worlds. *Philosophy and Phenomenological Research* **97**: 367–392.

Crummett, D. (2017) Sufferer-centered requirements on theodicy and all-things-considered harms. *Oxford Studies in Philosophy of Religion* **8**: 71–95.

Crummett, D. (2019) Review of Kraay, K., ed. *Does God Matter: Essays on the Axiological Consequences of Theism. Faith and Philosophy* **36**: 396–402.

Daeley, J. (2019) The necessity of the best possible world, divine thankworthi-ness, and grace. *Sophia* **58**: 423–435.

Davis, R. and Franks, W.P. (2015) Counterpossibles and the "terrible" divine command deity. *Religious Studies* **51**: 1–19.

Davis, S. T. (2014) On preferring that God not exist (or that God exist): a dialogue. *Faith and Philosophy* **31**: 143–159.

Davison, S. (1997) Privacy and control. *Faith and Philosophy* **14**: 137–151.

Davison, S. (2018) God and intrinsic value. In K. J. Kraay, *ed., Does God Matter? Essays on the Axiological Consequences of Theism.* New York: Routledge, pp. 39–45.

Diller, J. and Kasher, A. (2013) *Models of God and Alternative Ultimate Realities.* Dordrecht: Springer.

Dreier, J. (2004) Why ethical satisficing makes sense and rational satisficing doesn't. In M. Byron, *ed., Satisficing and Maximizing: Moral Theorists on Practical Reason.* Cambridge: Cambridge University Press, pp. 131–154.

Dumsday, T. (2016) Anti-theism and the problem of divine hiddenness. *Sophia* **55**: 179–195.

Dumsday, T. (2020) The axiology of theism: expanding the contrast classes. In K. Lougheed, *ed., Four Views on the Axiology of Theism: What Difference Does God Make?* London: Bloomsbury, pp. 59–78.

Elliot, D. and Soifer, E. (2017) Divine omniscience, privacy, and the state. *International Journal for Philosophy of Religion* **82**: 251–271.

Evans, C. S. (2013) *God and Moral Obligation.* Oxford: Oxford University Press.

Fales, E. (1994) Divine freedom and the choice of a world. *International Journal for Philosophy of Religion* **35**: 65–88.

Falls-Corbitt, M. and McLain, F. M. (1992) God and privacy. *Faith and Philosophy* **9**: 369–386.

Flint, T. P. (1983) The problem of divine freedom. *American Philosophical Quarterly* **20**: 255–264.

Forrest, P. (1981) The problem of evil: two neglected defences. *Sophia* **20**: 49–54.

Gellman, J. (2010) On God, suffering, and theodical individualism. *European Journal for Philosophy of Religion* **1**: 187–191.

Grover, S. (1988) Why only the best is good enough. *Analysis* **48**: 224.

Grover, S. (2003) This world, "Adams worlds," and the best of all possible worlds. *Religious Studies* **39**: 145–163.

Grover, S. (2004) Rival creator arguments and the best of all possible worlds. *Sophia* **43**: 101–114.

Guleserian, T. (1983) God and possible worlds: the modal problem of evil. *Noûs* **17**: 221–238.

Hall, R. L. (2020) On being known: God and the private-I. *Sophia* **59**: 621–636.

Hallett, G. (2001) The tedium of immortality. *Faith and Philosophy* **18**: 279–291.

Hare, J. (2015) *God's Command*. Oxford: Oxford University Press.

Hasker, W. (1992) The necessity of gratuitous evil. *Faith and Philosophy* **9**: 23–44.

Hasker, W. (2004) Can God permit "just enough" evil? In W. Hasker, *ed. Providence, Evil, and The Openness of God*. New York: Routledge, pp. 81–94.

Hasker, W. (2008) *The Triumph of God over Evil: Theodicy for a World of Suffering*. Downers Grove, IL: InterVarsity Press.

Hasker W. (2019) God and gratuitous evil: a response to Klaas Kraay. *Oxford Studies in Philosophy of Religion* **9**: 54–67.

Hedberg, T. and Huzarevich, J. (2017) Appraising objections to practical apatheism. *Philosophia* **45**: 257–276.

Hendricks, P. (2020) Skeptical theism, pro-theism, and anti-theism. In K. Lougheed, *ed., Four Views on the Axiology of Theism: What Difference Does God Make?* London: Bloomsbury, pp. 95–115.

Hendricks, P. and Lougheed, K. (2019) Undermining the axiological solution to divine hiddenness. *International Journal for Philosophy of Religion* **86**: 3–15.

Howard-Snyder, D. (1996) The argument from divine hiddenness. *Canadian Journal of Philosophy* **26**: 433–453.

Howard-Snyder, D. and Green, A. (2016) Hiddenness of God. In E. Zalta, *ed. Stanford Encyclopedia of Philosophy* (Winter 2016 Edition), https://plato.stanford.edu/archives/win2016/entries/divine-hiddenness/.

Johnson, D. K. (2014) The failure of the multiverse hypothesis as a solution to the problem of no best world. *Sophia* **53**: 447–465.

Johnston, M. (2019) Why did the one not remain within itself? *Oxford Studies in Philosophy of Religion* **9**: 106–164.

Jordan, J. (2003) Evil and Van Inwagen. *Faith and Philosophy* **20**: 236–239.

Jordan, J. (2004) Divine love and human suffering. *International Journal for Philosophy of Religion* **56**: 169–178.

Kahane, G. (2011) Should we want God to exist? *Philosophy and Phenomenological Research* **82**: 674–696.

Kahane, G. (2014) Our cosmic insignificance. *Noûs* **48**: 745–772.

Kahane, G. (2018) If there is a hole, it is not God-shaped. In Kraay, K., *ed.*, *Does God Matter? Essays on the Axiological Consequences of Theism*. New York: Routledge, pp. 95–131.

Kahane, G. (forthcoming) Is anti-theism incoherent? *American Philosophical Quarterly*.

Kant, I. (1978) *Lectures on Philosophical Theology. Trans.* A. W. Wood and G. M. Clark. Ithaca, NY: Cornell University Press.

Kraal, A. (2013) Is the existence of the best possible world logically impossible? *International Philosophical Quarterly* **53**: 37–46.

Kraay, K. J. (2008a) Can God choose a world at random? In E. Wielenberg and Y. Nagasawa, *eds.*, *New Waves in Philosophy of Religion*. New York: Palgrave Macmillan, 22–35.

Kraay, K. J. (2008b) Creation, world-actualization, and God's choice among possible worlds. *Philosophy Compass* **3**: 854–872.

Kraay, K. J. (2010a) The problem of no best world. In C. Taliaferro, P. Draper, and P. Quinn, *eds.*, *A Companion to Philosophy of Religion* (2nd ed.), Oxford: Wiley-Blackwell, pp. 481–491.

Kraay K. J. (2010b) Theism, possible worlds, and the multiverse. *Philosophical Studies* **147**: 355–368.

Kraay, K. J. (2011) Theism and modal collapse. *American Philosophical Quarterly* **48**: 361–372.

Kraay, K. J. (2012) The theistic multiverse: problems and prospects. In Nagasawa, Y., *ed.*, *Scientific Approaches to the Philosophy of Religion*. New York: Palgrave Macmillan, pp. 143–162.

Kraay, K. J. (2013a) Can God satisfice? *American Philosophical Quarterly* **50**: 399–410.

Kraay, K. J. (2013b) The problem of divine hiddenness. *Oxford Bibliographies Online*. www.oxfordbibliographies.com/view/document/obo-9780195396577/obo-9780195396577–0178.xml.

Kraay, K. J. (2014) Peter van Inwagen on gratuitous evil. *Religious Studies* **50**: 217–234.

Kraay, K. J., *ed.* (2015) *God and the Multiverse: Scientific, Philosophical, and Theological Perspectives*. New York: Routledge.

Kraay, K. J. (2018a) Invitation to the axiology of theism. In K. J. Kraay, *ed.*, *Does God Matter? Essays on the Axiological Consequences of Theism*. New York: Routledge, pp. 1–36.

Kraay, K. J. (2018b) One philosopher's bug can be another's feature: reply to Almeida's "Multiverse and Divine Creation." *Religions* **9**: 55–63.

Kraay, K. J. (2019) Theism, pro-theism, Hasker, and gratuitous evil. *Oxford Studies in Philosophy of Religion* **9**: 31–53.

Kraay, K. J. (forthcoming) Is motivated submaximization good enough for God? *Religious Studies*.

Kraay, K. J. and Dragos, C. (2013) On preferring God's non-existence. *Canadian Journal of Philosophy* **43**: 153–178.

Kretzmann, N. (1990a) A general problem of creation: why would God create anything at all? In S. McDonald, *ed.*, *Being and Goodness*. Ithaca, NY: Cornell University Press, pp. 208–228.

Kretzmann, N. (1990b) A particular problem of creation: why would God create this world? In S. McDonald, *ed.*, *Being and Goodness*. Ithaca, NY: Cornell University Press, pp. 229–249.

Lackey, D. P. (1985) Divine omniscience and human privacy. *Philosophy Research Archives* **10**: 383–391.

Leftow, B. 2005. The ontological argument. In W. Wainwright, *ed.*, *The Oxford Handbook of Philosophy of Religion*. New York: Oxford University Press, pp. 80–115.

Leftow, B. 2010. Necessity. In C. Taliaferro and C. Meister, *eds.*, *The Cambridge Companion to Philosophical Theology*. Cambridge: Cambridge University Press, pp. 15–30.

Leftow, B. 2017. Two pictures of divine choice. In H. J. McCann, *ed.*, *Free Will and Classical Theism: The Significance of Perfect Being Theology*. Oxford: Oxford University Press, pp. 152–172.

Leftow, B. (forthcoming) Divine freedom. In J. Campbell, *ed.*, *The Wiley Companion to Free Will*. Oxford: Wiley-Blackwell.

Leibniz, G. W. (1902) *Discourse on Metaphysics. Trans.* G. Montgomery. La Salle: Open Court.

Leibniz, G. W. (1986) *Theodicy. Ed.* A. Farrer. , *Trans.* E. M. Huggard. La Salle: Open Court.

Lewis, D. (1986) *On the Plurality of Worlds*. Oxford: Blackwell.

Lewis, D. (1993) Evil for freedom's sake? *Philosophical Papers* **22**: 149–172.

Licon, J. (forthcoming) Aspirational theism and gratuitous suffering. *Religious Studies*.

Lougheed, K. (2017) Anti-theism and the objective meaningful life argument. *Dialogue* **56**: 337–355.

Lougheed, K. (2018a) The axiological solution to divine hiddenness. *Ratio* **31**: 331–341.

Lougheed, K. (2018b) On the axiology of a hidden god. *European Journal for Philosophy of Religion* **10**: 79–95.

Lougheed, K. (2019) The axiology of theism. In J. Feiser and B. Dowden, *eds.*, *Internet Encyclopedia of Philosophy*, https://iep.utm.edu/axio-thei/.

Lougheed, K., ed. (2020a) *Four Views on the Axiology of Theism: What Difference Does God Make?* London: Bloomsbury.

Lougheed, K. (2020b) *The Axiological Status of Theism and Other Worldviews*. New York: Palgrave Macmillan.

Lovejoy, A. O. (1936) *The Great Chain of Being*. Boston, MA: Harvard University Press.

Lovering, R. (2011) Does ordinary morality imply atheism? A reply to Maitzen. *Forum Philosophicum* **16**: 83–98.

Mackie, J. L. (1955) Evil and omnipotence. *Mind* **64**: 200–212.

Maitzen, S. (2009) Ordinary morality implies atheism. *European Journal for Philosophy of Religion* **1**: 107–126.

Maitzen, S. (2010) On Gellman's attempted rescue. *European Journal for Philosophy of Religion* **2**: 193–198.

Maitzen, S. (2013) Atheism and the basis of morality. In A. W. Musschenga and A. van Harskamp, *eds.*, *What Makes Us Moral?* Dordrecht: Springer, pp. 257–269.

Maitzen, S. (2018) The Problem of Magic. In K. Kraay. *Does God Matter? Essays on the Axiological Consequences of Theism*. New York: Routledge, pp. 132–146.

Maitzen, S. (2019) Normative objections to theism. In G. Oppy, *ed.*, *A Companion to Atheism and Philosophy*, Oxford: Wiley Blackwell, pp. 204–215.

Manson, N. A., *ed.* (2003) *God and Design: The Teleological Argument and Modern Science*. London: Routledge.

Martin, M. and Monnier, R., *eds.*, (2003) *The Impossibility of God*. Amherst, NY: Prometheus Books.

Mawson, T.J. (2011) Theodical individualism. *European Journal for Philosophy of Religion* **3**: 139–159.

Mawson, T.J. (2012). On determining how important it is whether or not there is a God. *European Journal for Philosophy of Religion* **4**: 95–105.

Mawson, T.J. (2016) *God and the Meanings of Life*. New York: Bloomsbury.

Mawson, T.J. (2018) An agreeable answer to a pro-theism/anti-theism question. In K. Kraay, *ed.*, *Does God Matter? Essays on the Axiological Consequences of Theism*. New York: Routledge, pp. 70–92.

McBrayer, J. and Howard-Snyder, D., *eds.*, (2013) *The Blackwell Companion to The Problem of Evil*. Malden, MA: Wiley-Blackwell.

McKim, R. (2001) *Religious Ambiguity and Religious Diversity*. Oxford: Oxford University Press.

Menzel, C. (2016) Possible worlds. In E. Zalta, *ed.*, *Stanford Encyclopedia of Philosophy* (Winter 2017 ed.), https://plato.stanford.edu/archives/win2017/entries/possible-worlds/.

Metz. T. (2013a) The meaning of life. In E. Zalta, *ed.*, *Stanford Encyclopedia of Philosophy* (Summer 2013 ed.), https://plato.stanford.edu/archives/sum2013/entries/life-meaning/.

Metz, T. (2013b) *Meaning in Life: An Analytic Study.* Oxford: Oxford University Press.

Metz, T. (2019) *God, Soul, and the Meaning of Life.* Cambridge: Cambridge University Press.

Morris, T. (1987) The necessity of God's goodness. In *Anselmian Explorations: Essays in Philosophical Theology.* Notre Dame, IN: University of Notre Dame Press, pp. 42–69.

Moser, P. (2013) On the axiology of theism: reply to Klaas J. Kraay. *Toronto Journal of Theology* **29**: 271–276.

Mulgan, T. (2001) How satisficers get away with murder. *International Journal of Philosophical Studies* **9**: 41–6.

Murphy, M. (2011) *God and Moral Law: On the Theistic Explanation of Morality.* Oxford: Oxford University Press.

Murray, M. (2002) Deus absconditus. In D. Howard-Snyder and P. Moser, *eds.*, *Divine Hiddenness: New Essays.* Cambridge, UK: Cambridge University Press, pp. 62–82.

Nagasawa, Y. (forthcoming) Pro-immortalism and pro-mortalism. In T. R. Byerly, *ed.*, *Death, Immortality, and Eternal Life.* London: Routledge.

Naylor, M. (2020) Satisfactory accounts of divine creation. *International Journal for Philosophy of Religion* **88**: 249–258.

Nelson, M. (1996) Who are the best judges of theistic arguments? *Sophia* **35**: 1–12.

Nielsen, K. (1973) *Ethics without God.* Buffalo, NY: Prometheus Books.

O'Connor, D. (1998) *God and Inscrutable Evil: In Defense of Theism and Atheism*, Lanham, MD: Rowman and Littlefield.

Oppy, G. (1998) Judging theistic arguments. *Sophia* **37**: 30–43.

Oppy. G. (2020) Naturalistic axiology. In K. Lougheed, *ed.*, *Four Views on the Axiology of Theism.* London: Bloomsbury, pp. 138–155.

Penner, M. A. (2015) Personal anti-theism and the meaningful life argument. *Faith and Philosophy* **32**: 325–337.

Penner, M. A. (2018) On the objective meaningful life argument: a response to Kirk Lougheed. *Dialogue* 57: 173–182.

Penner, M.A. and Lougheed, K. (2015). Pro-theism and the added value of morally good agents. *Philosophia Christi* **17**: 53–69.

Plantinga, A. (1974a) *God, Freedom, and Evil*. New York: Harper and Row.

Plantinga, A. (1974b) *The Nature of Necessity*. Oxford: Clarendon Press.

Plantinga, A. (2004) Supralapsarianism, or "O Felix Culpa." In P. van Inwagen, ed., *Christian Faith and the Problem of Evil*. Grand Rapids: Eerdmans, pp. 1–25.

Plato. (1980) *Euthyphro. Trans.* L. Cooper. In E. Hamilton and H. Cairns, *eds. The Collected Dialogues of Plato, Including the Letters*. Princeton, NJ: Princeton University Press, pp. 169–185

Plato. (1980) *Timaeus. Trans.* B. Jowett. In E. Hamilton and H. Cairns, *eds. The Collected Dialogues of Plato, Including the Letters*. Princeton, NJ: Princeton University Press, pp. 1151–1211.

Pollock, J. (1983) How do you maximize expectation value? *Noûs* **17**: 409–21.

Quinn, P. L. (1978) *Divine Commands and Moral Requirements*. Oxford: Clarendon Press.

Quinn, P. L. (1982). God, moral perfection, and possible worlds. In F. Sontag and M.D. Bryant, *eds., God: The Contemporary Discussion*. New York: The Rose of Sharon Press, pp. 197–213.

Rasmussen, J. and Leon, F. (2019) *Is God the Best Explanation of Things? A Dialogue*. New York: Palgrave Macmillan.

Reichenbach, B. (1982) *Evil and a Good God*. New York: Fordham University Press.

Rescher, N. (1990) On faith and belief. In *Human Interests: Reflections on Philosophical Anthropology*. Stanford, CA: Stanford University Press, pp. 167–178.

Richardson, H.S. (1994) Satisficing: not good enough. In M. Byron, *ed., Satisficing and Maximizing: Moral Theorists on Practical Reason*. Cambridge: Cambridge University Press, pp. 106–130.

Rowe, W.L. (1979) The problem of evil and some varieties of atheism. *American Philosophical Quarterly* **16**: 335–341.

Rowe, W.L. (1993) The problem of divine perfection and freedom. In E. Stump, *ed., Reasoned Faith*. Ithaca, NY: Cornell University Press, pp. 223–233.

Rowe, W.L. (1996) William Alston on the problem of evil. In T. Senor, *ed., The Rationality of Belief and the Plurality of Faiths*. Cornell, NY: Cornell University Press, pp. 71–93.

Rowe, W.L. (2004) *Can God be Free?* Oxford: Oxford University Press.

Rowe, W.L. and Kraay K. (forthcoming) Divine freedom. *Stanford Encyclopedia of Philosophy*.

Rubio, D. (2020) In defence of no best world. *Australasian Journal of Philosophy* **98**: 811–825.

Schellenberg, J. L. (1993) *Divine Hiddenness and Human Reason*. Ithaca, NY: Cornell University Press.

Schellenberg, J. L. (2007) *The Wisdom to Doubt: A Justification of Religious Skepticism*. Ithaca, NY: Cornell University Press.

Schellenberg, J. L. (2015) *The Hiddenness Argument: Philosophy's New Challenge to Belief in God*. Oxford: Oxford University Press.

Schellenberg, J.L. (2018) Triple transcendence, the value of God's existence, and a new route to atheism. In K. Kraay, *ed.*, *Does God Matter? Essays on the Axiological Consequences of Theism*. New York: Routledge, pp. 181–191.

Schlesinger, G. (1977) *Religion and Scientific Method*. Dordrecht, Reidel.

Schmidtz, D. (2004) Satisficing as a humanly rational strategy. In M. Byron, *ed.*, *Satisficing and Maximizing: Moral Theorists on Practical Reason*. Cambridge: Cambridge University Press, pp. 30–58.

Seachris, J., *ed.* (2013). *Exploring the Meaning of Life: An Anthology and Guide*. Malden, MA: Wiley: Blackwell.

Seachris, J. and Goetz, S. (2020) *What is This Thing called The Meaning of Life?* New York: Routledge.

Senor, T. (2008) Defending divine freedom. *Oxford Studies in Philosophy of Religion* **1**: 168–195.

Slote, M. (1989) *Beyond Optimizing: A Study of Rational Choice*. Cambridge: Harvard University Press.

Sobel, J.H. (2004) *Logic and Theism: Arguments for and against Beliefs in God*. Cambridge: Cambridge University Press.

Sorensen, R. (1994) Infinite decision theory. In J. Jordan., *ed.*, *Gambling with God: Essays on Pascal's Wager*. Totowa, NJ: Rowman & Littlefield, pp. 139–159.

Sorensen, R. (2006) Originless sin: a rational dilemma for satisficers. *Philosophical Quarterly* **56**: 213–223.

Stump, E. (1990) Providence and the problem of evil. In T. Flint, *ed.* *Christian Philosophy*. Notre Dame: University of Notre Dame Press, pp. 51–91.

Stump, E. (2010) *Wandering In Darkness: Narrative and the Problem of Suffering*. Oxford: Oxford University Press.

Swinburne, R. (2004) *The Existence of God* (2nd ed.). Oxford: Clarendon Press.

Swinburne, R. (2016) *The Coherence of Theism* (2nd ed.). Oxford: Clarendon Press.

Swinburne, R. (1998) *Providence and the Problem of Evil*. Oxford: Clarendon Press.

Talbott, T. (2014) *The Inescapable Love of God*. Eugene, OR: Cascade Books.

Taliaferro, C. (1989) Does God violate your right to privacy? *Theology* **92**: 190–196.

Tooley, M. (1991) The argument from evil. *Philosophical Perspectives* **5**: 88–134.

Tooley, M. (2018) Axiology: theism versus widely accepted monotheisms. In K. Kraay, *ed.*, *Does God Matter? Essays on the Axiological Consequences of Theism*. New York: Routledge, pp. 46–69.

Tucker, C. (2016) Satisficing and motivated submaximization (in the philosophy of religion). *Philosophy and Phenomenological Research* **93**: 127–143.

Ullman-Margalit, E. and Morganbesser, S. (1977) Picking and choosing. *Social Research* **44**: 757–785.

Vaidya, A. (2015) The epistemology of modality. In E. Zalta, *ed. Stanford Encyclopedia of Philosophy* (Winter 2017 ed.), https://plato.stanford.edu/archives/win2017/entries/modality-epistemology/.

Van Inwagen, P. (1988) The place of chance in a world sustained by God. In T. V. Morris, *ed.*, *Divine and Human Action*. Ithaca, NY: Cornell University Press, pp. 211–235.

Van Inwagen, P. (1998) Modal epistemology. *Philosophical Studies* **92**: 67–84.

Van Inwagen, P. (2006) *The Problem of Evil*. Oxford: Oxford University Press.

Wainwright, W. (2005) *Religion and Morality*. Aldershot: Ashgate.

Walls, J. (1992) *Hell: The Logic of Damnation*. South Bend: University of Notre Dame Press.

Walls, J. (2007) *Heaven: The Logic of Eternal Joy*. Oxford: Oxford University Press.

Wielenberg, E. (2004) A morally unsurpassable God must create the best. *Religious Studies* **40**: 43–62.

Wielenberg, E. (2005) *Value and Virtue in a Godless Universe*. Cambridge: Cambridge University Press.

Wielenberg, E. (2018) The absurdity of life in a Christian universe as a reason to prefer that God not exist. In K. Kraay, *ed.*, *Does God Matter? Essays on the Axiological Consequences of Theism*. New York: Routledge, pp. 147–163.

Wierenga, E. (2002) The freedom of God. *Faith and Philosophy* **19**: 425–436.

Williams, B. (1973) The Makropulos case: reflections on the tedium of immortality. In *Problems of the Self*. Cambridge: Cambridge University Press, pp. 82–100.

Wykstra, S. (1984) The Humean obstacle to evidential arguments from suffering: on avoiding the evils of 'appearance.' *International Journal for Philosophy of Religion* **16**: 73–93.

Zagzebski, L. (2008) Omnisubjectivity. *Oxford Studies in Philosophy of Religion* **1**: 231–248.

Zagzebski, L. (2013) *Omnisubjectivity: A Defense of a Divine Attribute.* Milwaukee, WI: Marquette University Press.

Zagzebski, L. (2016) Omnisubjectivity: why it is a divine attribute. *Nova et Vetera* **14**: 435–450.

Zagzebski, L. (2017) Foreknowledge and free will. In E. Zalta, *ed., Stanford Encyclopedia of Philosophy* (Summer 2017 ed.), https://plato.stanford.edu /archives/sum2017/entries/free-will-foreknowledge/.

Acknowledgments

I am grateful to Yujin Nagasawa for the opportunity to write this Element. I am thankful to the John Templeton Foundation for generously funding my research project entitled "Theism: An Axiological Investigation" from 2013 to 2015. (The project website is https://people.ryerson.ca/kraay/theism.html.) This allowed me to begin the systematic work that culminated in this Element. The project also supported four visiting research fellows: Richard Brian Davis, Myron A. Penner, W. Paul Franks, and Toby Betenson. I'm grateful to each of them for many invigorating conversations about this topic. I'm very thankful for the outstanding research climate at Ryerson University, and also for the generous research support I received while on sabbatical in 2020 from (i) the Studiecentrum Oud Rustenburg; (ii) the Faculty of Religion and Theology; and (iii) the CLUE+ Institute at the Vrije Universiteit Amsterdam. Special thanks are due to Dirk-Martin Grube and to René van Woudenberg for making my time at "de VU" so intellectually stimulating, despite the challenges of COVID-19. I'm grateful to Jeroen de Ridder, Chris Ranalli, Rik Peels, and René van Woudenberg for incisive and detailed feedback on Section 2. I'm particularly thankful to Kirk Lougheed, and to an anonymous referee, for extremely helpful feedback on the entire manuscript. I am profoundly grateful to my wife, Mary Beth, and our two children, Emma and Jacob, for their unconditional love and support. Finally, I'm very thankful to our wonderful nephew and neice, Alex Kraay and Isabella Kraay, for providing much-needed babysitting during my final push to complete this manuscript!

For my mother, Gerardina Adriana Kraay-Hofman (1935–2019).
I inherited her deep desire to think carefully about God.

Cambridge Elements ⹀

Philosophy of Religion

Yujin Nagasawa
University of Birmingham

Yujin Nagasawa is Professor of Philosophy and Co-director of the John Hick Centre for Philosophy of Religion at the University of Birmingham. He is currently President of the British Society for the Philosophy of Religion. He is a member of the Editorial Board of *Religious Studies*, the *International Journal for Philosophy of Religion*, and *Philosophy Compass*.

About the Series

This Cambridge Elements series provides concise and structured introductions to all the central topics in the philosophy of religion. It offers balanced, comprehensive coverage of multiple perspectives in the philosophy of religion. Contributors to the series are cutting-edge researchers who approach central issues in the philosophy of religion. Each provides a reliable resource for academic readers and develops new ideas and arguments from a unique viewpoint.

Cambridge Elements≡

Philosophy of Religion

Elements in the Series

A full series listing is available at: www.cambridge.org/EPREL

Printed in the United States
by Baker & Taylor Publisher Services

Printed in the United States
by Baker & Taylor Publisher Services